BEYOND CAPITALISM

The Japanese Model of Market Economics

Eisuke Sakakibara

With an Introduction by
Clyde V. Prestowitz, Jr.

UNIVERSITY
PRESS OF
AMERICA

Lanham • New York • London

ECONOMIC
STRATEGY
INSTITUTE

Copyright © 1993 by the
Economic Strategy Institute

University Press of America®, Inc.
4720 Boston Way
Lanham, Maryland 20706

3 Henrietta Street
London WC2E 8LU England

Co-published by arrangement with the
Economic Strategy Institute

Library of Congress Cataloging-in-Publication Data

Sakakibara, Eisuke.
Beyond capitalism : the Japanese model of market
economics / by Eisuke Sakakibara ; with an
introduction by Clyde V. Prestowitz, Jr.
p.   cm.
"Co-published by arrangement with the
Economic Strategy Institute"—T.p. verso.
Includes bibliographical references.
1. Japan—Economic conditions.   2. Japan—
Economic policy.   3. Capitalism—Japan.
4. Mixed economy—Japan.   I. Title.
HC462.9.S19255   1993
330.952—dc20   93–6476 CIP

ISBN 0–8191–9061–6 (cloth : alk. paper)
ISBN 0–8191–9062–4 (pbk. : alk. paper)

 The paper used in this publication meets the minimum requirements of
American National Standard for Information Sciences—Permanence
of Paper for Printed Library Materials, ANSI Z39.48–1984.

TABLE OF CONTENTS

Preface to the English Edition

Approximately three years have passed since I published the Japanese version of this book. Much has taken place during these three years but the issue I raised--that of different capitalisms--seems to have come to the forefront of various policy discussions. As Clyde Prestowitz points out in his introduction, the assertion that Japanese capitalism--or what I call a non-capitalist market economy--is different from other forms has been framed in the context of the debate between "traditionalists" and "revisionists" over the Japanese economy.

Today, I think we could analyze the subject in the much wider context of different capitalisms the world over. A neo-classical, or neo-American, view of capitalism, which dominated the world in the decade of the 1980s, seems to have passed its peak. Authors such as Robert Kuttner declare the second end of "laissez-faire." The post-socialist age may also become a post laissez-faire age.

Indeed, as Michel Albert argued in his recent book, *Capitalisme contre Capitalisme,* Anglo-Saxon or neo-American capitalism may be sharing the world with a continental European model--which he calls the Rhine-Alpen model--as well as with a Japanese or East Asian model. Although I do not go into comparative analyses of these different models of capitalism, I wish to emphasize in this book that there is, at least, one legitimate model of capitalism that is different from the American or neo-classical economic model.

Whether we call it capitalism or not is a matter of semantics. To the extent that the Japanese system is based on the principle of private ownership of factors of production and dominated by private incorporated companies, it could very well be called capitalism. Yet to the extent that capitalists do not dominate the economy and typical firms are based on the principle of employee sovereignty, it could also be classified as a non-capitalistic regime. Although I called the Japanese system a non-capitalistic market economy in this book, I would not mind renaming it Japanese capitalism, as long as different versions of capitalism are recognized as legitimate alternatives that a country may choose or develop according to its own historical and cultural evolution.

Taking this pluralistic position that capitalisms can differ across national borders and according to various historical and cultural backgrounds, our views on the world economy and world trade should be transformed as well. Indeed, in this increasingly interdependent world, many aspects of different national economies need to be harmonized. Yet to the extent that different regimes continue to be different, they will have to accommodate each other in certain ways. In some instances, these accommodations may take the form of modification of the principle of laissez-faire. The governments in question will have to negotiate and find mutually satisfactory ways to intervene in response to market failures. In an imperfect world with asymmetrical information availability and differing institutional arrangements, government interventions can be useful, although market mechanisms should still remain the primary channel of resource allocation.

The management of external policies in this truly pluralistic world should be more pragmatic and less ideological. And it should seek new, non-laissez-faire rules that still are primarily market-oriented. This is the challenge that all of us in the increasingly integrated world face in the 1990s, when a new paradigm that transcends both the new conservatism and the principle of laissez-faire will have to be firmly established.

Introduction

by Clyde V. Prestowitz, Jr.

Is Japan different? More specifically, is the Japanese economy based on significantly different principles than is America's?

Until the mid-1980s, these questions were mainly of academic interest--and not even many scholars seemed to care. More recently, they have moved to the center of the vigorous debate over how America should respond to the challenge presented by growing Japanese economic strength, and the related controversy over how the United States can revitalize its own economy.

In fact, whether or not Japan is different will have an increasingly important impact on the future of the entire global economy. It will help determine the rules by which international commerce is conducted and the development strategies pursued by third world countries and the former communist states, and it will bear critically on the issue of whether the long international economic peace that has held in the non-communist world since the end of World War II will last.

The Revisionists

Thus far, the portion of the debate that has attracted the most attention has been conducted mainly by Americans. The controversy was triggered by the writings of a small group of analysts who have come to be known as the "revisionists." They see the Japanese economy as being based on principles and having objectives, structures, and operating practices that deviate very substantially from the neo-classical Western capitalist model. In their view, U.S.-Japanese frictions stem ultimately from a clash of two very different systems that is unlikely to be ameliorated by the application of general rules on which the two countries simply do not agree.[1]

The basics of the revisionist argument can be summarized as follows: U.S. economic policy focuses on consumption as the primary engine of economic growth and seeks to maximize consumer welfare at any given moment. Indeed, much consumption is either subsidized or taxed very lightly, while interest earned on savings, investment, and capital gains is taxed relatively heavily or otherwise penalized. National security is seen to be related to economic policy only in the narrow sense of maintaining the capability to manufacture weapons.

Japan, by contrast, has emphasized production as the means of assuring sustained economic growth. In Japan consumption is taxed while production is treated favorably. The Japanese believe that promoting production is the best way to ensure long-term increases in living standards--that consumers will not be able to consume unless they produce. Moreover, Japan has tightly linked economic policy and national security ever since Commodore Perry steamed into Tokyo Bay. This has been particularly true in the post-World War II period, when Japan, having constitutionally renounced military force as an instrument of national power, has defined national security almost exclusively in economic terms. A recent expression of this is MITI's *Vision of Japan for the 1990s,* which speaks of achieving technological autonomy and bargaining power with other nations through technological and industrial leadership.

These differences in fundamental economic objectives have given rise to two dramatically different philosophies with regard to the structure of the economy. Because the United States does not concern itself much with production, it has no view as to what it is best to produce and adopts a largely laissez-faire attitude toward economic structure. This is reflected in the question posed in 1985 by then Deputy Treasury Secretary Richard Darman in response to complaints of foreign dumping of semiconductor chips in the U.S. market: "Why do we want a

---

[1]The principal revisionist works include Pat Choate, *Agents of Influence: How Japan's Lobbyists in the United States Manipulate America's Political and Economic System* (Knopf, 1990); James Fallows, "Containing Japan," *The Atlantic,* May, 1989; Chalmers Johnson, *MITI and the Japanese Miracle: The Growth of Industrial Policy, 1925-1975* (Stanford University Press, 1982); Clyde V. Prestowitz, Jr., *Trading Places: How We Allowed Japan to Take the Lead* (Basic Books, 1988); and Karen G. van Wolferen, *The Enigma of Japanese Power: People and Politics in a Stateless Nation* (Knopf, 1989). Choate, Fallows, Prestowitz, and van Wolferen co-authored a short, convenient summary of revisionism in 1990. See "Beyond Japan-bashing: `The Gang of Four' Defends the Revisionist Line," *U.S. News and World Report,* May 7, 1990.

semiconductor industry? If our guys can't hack it, let them go."[2]   It is inconceivable that Darman's Japanese counterpart would make such a statement. Since the time of Meiji, according to the reknowned Canadian Japanologist E.H. Norman, the Japanese "were concerned with such questions as establishing those industries which one might conveniently call strategic."[3] In the post-war period, they have emphasized development of capital-intensive, high technology, high value-added industries and have passed legislation and pursued industrial policies explicitly aimed at gaining leadership in key industries. This observation was confirmed in the late 1970s by a study group appointed by then-Prime Minister Masayoshi Ohira to analyze the secrets of Japan's past success in order to ensure continued future success. The group noted that the Japanese government is an integral part of the "collegial groups" that constitute the Japanese economy, and that its role in assuring an optimum structure for the Japanese economy is critical. Thus the development of economic "visions" and the use of administrative guidance to achieve them are among the most important activities of Japanese policy makers. This is in stark contrast to the view held by American neo-classical economists, which can be summed up in the phrase, "Potato chips, computer chips; what's the difference? They're all chips."

Different attitudes on the importance of production and economic structure have in turn led to major differences between the financial environments and the related corporate structures fostered by the U.S. and Japanese systems. Three stand out, according to economist David Hale of Kemper Financial Services.

First is the fact that, unlike U.S. corporations, Japanese companies are not controlled by retail shareholders or financial institutions seeking to maximize profits through capital gains or dividends. Instead, two-thirds of the equity of Japanese corporations is held in the hands of other related corporations and friendly financial institutions in a cross shareholding network that has come to be described as a *keiretsu,* or economic alliance. The members of these *keiretsu* networks do not view their portfolios as passive investments, but as a means to enhance business relations as well as to prevent unwanted takeover bids. Indeed, as explained by Tokyo-based investment banker Robert Zielinski and financial journalist Nigel Holloway, "From the viewpoint of investors, the Japanese

---

[2]Quoted in Clyde V. Prestowitz, Jr., "Tools--Not Hula Hoops," *Washington Post*, December 3, 1991.

[3]E. H. Norman, *Origins of the Modern Japanese State: Selected Writings of E. H. Norman,* John Dower, ed. (Pantheon, 1975), p. 225.

corporation is almost impervious to outside influence."[4] Of course, such cross shareholding networks would be illegal in the United States for precisely this reason.

The second major difference noted by Hale is the role played by the Japanese shareholding system in helping to reduce the after-tax cost of capital for Japanese firms as compared to that of firms operating under the U.S.-style ownership system. Says Hale:

> The fact that Japanese banks own about 25 percent of all equity and often have a close supervisory relationship with industrial firms has permitted them [the firms] to maintain much higher debt/equity ratios than American firms. As in the United States, the interest payments on such debt are tax deductible. Partly as a result of the limited supply of free stock on the Tokyo stock market, Japanese shares also have tended to sell at higher multiples than U.S. firms on the basis of both earnings per share and cash flow per share. During the Tokyo stock market boom of the late 1980s, Japanese multiples rose to a level five times as high as those in the United States on the basis of earnings per share and twice as high for cash flow multiples.

Finally, says Hale, as a result of this system, Japanese corporations have adopted a strategy of market-share maximization as opposed to the profit maximization approach of most U.S. companies. For example, in a *Business Week* survey of the world's 1,000 largest companies, Japanese firms had a return on equity of 8.6 percent as compared to 15.6 percent for U.S. firms. In the same manner, the sales margin for U.S. companies averages about 5.6 percent as compared to 2.4 percent for Japanese companies. It is these low profit requirements made possible by low capital costs that have spurred the aggressive market penetration for which Japanese industry has become famous.[5]

Not surprisingly, American and Japanese attitudes on the question of anti-trust are dramatically opposed as well. Historically, Americans have viewed any concentration of power with suspicion. Just as we have created a system of checks and balances to prevent excessive accumulation of political power, so have we devised strict anti-trust regulations to prevent concentration of too much economic power. Moreover, we put real teeth into these regulations by enabling private

---

[4]Robert Zielinski and Nigel Holloway, *Unequal Equities: Power and Risk in Japan's Stock Market* (Kodansha International, 1991), p. 7.

[5]David Hale, "Will Rising Capital Costs Alter Japanese Corporate Behavior?" Congressional Budget Office, unpublished, June 23, 1992.

citizens as well as the government to initiate suits and by applying triple damages to those convicted of wrongdoing. Thus, U.S. corporations are prevented from fixing prices and maintaining resale prices as well as from controlling the activities of their dealers and distributors. As a consequence, the U.S. distribution system is essentially open to all sellers and has been a powerful factor in the penetration of the U.S. market by foreign producers by providing a ready sales channel to consumers.

Conversely, the Japanese not only have not feared concentrations of economic power, they have fostered them. During the occupation, the U.S. authorities introduced anti-trust rules similar to those in the United States and broke up the giant pre-war industrial conglomerates known as *zaibatsu*. Immediately after the occupation, however, the Japanese government moved quickly to water down the anti-trust regulations and to promote the concentration of Japanese companies into *keiretsu* that often bore the names of the old *zaibatsu*, such as Mitsui, Mitsubishi, and Sumitomo. Large Japanese corporations often engage in so-called *dango* activities that involve price fixing and bid rigging, and they rigidly control the activities of their dealers. For instance, unlike the case in the United States, in Japan auto dealers do not normally sell multiple brands. Rather, Toyota dealers sell Toyotas and Honda dealers sell Hondas, etc. Anti-trust complaints may be initiated only by the Japanese government, penalties are light, and the investigating staff is kept small and under-funded.

Indeed, according to the revisionists, different outlooks on economics can be seen across the board in the two systems--in macroeconomic policy, in their approaches toward research and development, in their attitudes toward structural adjustment, and in many other areas.

The revisionists emphasize that the existence of such differences does not imply that either system is "right" or "wrong," or that one is morally superior. And they acknowledge that many of America's economic problems are home-grown, and best solved through domestic change. Yet they maintain that the differences between the U.S. and Japanese economies nonetheless give rise to very real problems that must be dealt with if the two countries are to continue mutually beneficial relations.

The Traditionalists

The revisionists' arguments have been vigorously disputed by the "traditionalists"--Japan specialists and other commentators who insist that Japan's economy is essentially in the neo-classical Western mold, albeit with a few distinctively Japanese features. In this view, since, by definition there cannot be any systemic differences between the two economies, problems must be due to aberrations (usually identified as either poor performance by the Americans or cheating by the Japanese) that in theory can be addressed through negotiations and through the application of the universal principles of neo-classical free market economics.

In an April, 1992 speech in New York, for example, then-Vice President Dan Quayle attacked the idea "that Japan is radically different, that its corporations are not subject to normal market forces...." The Japanese economy, argued Quayle, is shaped "by the ebb and flow of normal economic forces...." Japanese corporations, are "subject to the same market forces as American or European companies." Echoing comments made by many other analysts, *Wall Street Journal* columnist Karen Elliott House wrote that same month that Japan's stock market slump shows that the Japanese "are demonstrably vulnerable to the same market forces that shape the economies of other mortals." Columbia University economist Jagdish Bhagwati in a January, 1992 essay cited "serious problems" with the "complex contention that Japanese institutions are so `different' that they effectively impede imports."

Sometimes such analysts go further, suggesting that Japan's economy is not only structurally identical to America's in most important ways, but that it embodies classic Western capitalist virtues more faithfully than America's. According to Melanie Kirkpatrick of *The Wall Street Journal*, Japan is "a country that has followed our model with the most spectacular success." "[A]ll of the things that you've been beating them over the head for are American values that they've adopted and you've forgotten about," claimed Dean George R. Packard of the Nitze School of Advanced International Studies in a December, 1989 televised debate with revisionist writer James Fallows.

Thus the traditionalists tend to conclude that Japan has succeeded economically simply because it practices Western-style capitalism better than anyone else. Said Packard, "[T]hey believe in hard work--Ben Franklin....they believe in savings. That's Dwight Eisenhower." Similarly, Charles Wolf, chief international economist for the Rand Corporation, wrote in a May, 1991 column that Japan's formidable record is largely due to "four simple factors": high investment rates, high savings rates, "highly disciplined, trained, industrious and literate" workers, and "energetic, competent and experienced managers."

Sometimes the traditionalists' arguments can be difficult to follow. For example, in his speech, Quayle maintained that although revisionism was understandable as recently as five years ago, "times have changed." He then proceeded to argue, variously, that "Japanese society is changing from within," that "this process is already underway," that "much more remains to be done," that foreign companies lack "reciprocal access to Japan's markets," and that "No one expects sweeping changes overnight." And all of these views must somehow be reconciled with the administration position that U.S. trade problems with Japan stem not only from conventional trade barriers but from "structural impediments" that require their own set of negotiations to eliminate.

In the televised debate, Packard described as "nonsense" the view that "Japan is somehow culturally or politically incapable of practicing free trade as we do" and blamed trade tensions on "a system set up by the United States and the government of Japan in the 1950s and 1960s...to protect their markets because we needed a Cold War ally." He also claimed that Japan "is changing very fast right now" and that "They're not changing fast enough."

What the Japanese Think

The passion of the debate is evident from the name-calling engaged in by both sides. The revisionists are often labeled "Japan bashers" and castigated for exaggerating differences between Japan and the West and their effects. Their secret agenda supposedly is excusing America's own economic shortcomings and justifying protectionist or discriminatory policies toward Japan. In response, the term "Chrysanthemum Club" is sometimes used to describe traditionalists who are criticized as apologists striving to explain every Japanese deviation from free market economics as a matter of Western businesses and governments failing adequately to understand Japan.

Yet the most striking aspect of this debate among Americans is that it is taking place at all. For the Japanese have long emphatically asserted that their post-World War II "economic miracle" has been based on rejection of the Western model and on the application of specifically Japanese precepts and methods. During the U.S. occupation, Western economists and Japan experts saw nothing but a small island country with no natural resources that had been shorn of the empire that had furnished both markets and raw materials. All Japan had in abundance was inexpensive labor, and the occupation advisers therefore urged that economic recovery be based on developing labor-intensive industries and attracting foreign capital investment. And even if this program were carried out in the most effective way, none expected more than minimal results. Indeed, as knowledgeable an observer as Edwin Reischauer, a Harvard professor who had been raised and educated in Japan by missionary parents and who was to be a future ambassador to Japan, wondered if Japan would ever have a satisfactory standard of living. As late as 1955, Secretary of State John Foster Dulles told Japanese officials that there "will always be an imbalance in Japan's direct trade with the U.S....." because of the shoddy goods Japan made.[6]

Beginning immediately from the end of the occupation, however, the Japanese rejected the Western advice and model. As declared by one of the architects of Japan's recovery, former Ministry of International Trade and Industry (MITI) Vice Minister Naohiro Amaya, "We violated all the traditional economic concepts....The realization of the myth that if you entrust things to the market mechanism, the invisible God's hand will bring about a rational result is quite limited."[7]

In other words, Adam Smith was not to be the model by which the Japanese miracle would be achieved. Post-war Japanese leaders' recognition of this reality was again made clear by Amaya, who said, "Post war Japan defined itself as a cultural state holding the principles of liberalism, democracy,and peace, but these were only superficial principles (tatemae); the fundamental objective (honne) was the pouring of all our strength into economic growth."[8]

The method by which this was done is described in a new book by University of Washington historian Kenneth B. Pyle titled *The Japanese Question.* Pyle points out that quasi-wartime controls were imposed on the financial system while the country was closed to foreign investment and domestic markets and industries were protected by high tariffs and rigid border controls. At the same time, the Japanese people were, in effect, forced to limit their consumption. The concentration of resources and the achievement of economies of scale in export-oriented industries took precedence over economic democracy. The principles and attitudes behind this program were well described by a MITI official who said in 1962:

> Free competition has a stifling effect on the economy. We must not allow it to be used in distributing the benefits of high growth-prices, wages, profits. We cannot pause to theorize about the sort of influence that a policy of concentration will have. If our export strength is assured, the growth of our economyis assured.[9]

---

[6]Jim Mann, "Eisenhower Weighed Asia Pullout in '50s, Files Show," *Los Angeles Times,* September 23, 1991.

[7]Prestowitz, *op. cit.,* p. 248.

[8]Quoted in Kenneth Pyle, *The Japanese Question: Power and Purpose in a New Era* (AEI Press, 1992), p. 36.

[9]Yoshihiko Morozumi as quoted in Daniel Okimoto and Thomas Rohlen, eds., *Inside the Japanese System: Readings on Contemporary Society and Political Economy* (Stanford University Press, 1988), p. 80.

By the late 1970s this prophecy had been fulfilled. The aforementioned Ohira study group emphasized that:

> Rather than encouraging intense competition among individuals, with each being wholly responsible for his actions, the Japanese economy relies on collegial groups that are based on various relationships created within and between companies. This tends to give rise to a phenomenon of dependence that is induced by mutual reliance among persons. In some instances, such a relationship can be detrimental to freedom and competition. However, the Japanese economy is the model which Western societies are now beginning to imitate.[10]

In explaining one of the key differences between the Japanese and Western models, the group noted that "In Japan, along with buyers and sellers in the market, the government too is a member of this collegial group, and the government does not have an adversary relationship with other participants in the market. Japan's administrative guidance functions extremely efficiently. Westerners often ask the reasons for success, and some of them, seeing it, use the phrase, `Japan, Inc.' " Amaya has further expanded on this analysis, explaining that

> Such...relationships are not only between a firm and its employees. They also exist between one firm and others with which it has business relationships, and between a firm and its banks. These inter-firm relationships are not cold, profit-loss relationships based on calculations and contracts, but cohesive relationships which have a large margin for emotion and sense of obligation.[11]

Suggestions that such relationships might tend to result in monopolistic practices that need to be regulated have been dismissed as ignorance of "the unique structure and ethics of Japanese society."

A Change of Tune

Thus for more than thirty years, Japan not only rejected the Western neo-classical model, but said so repeatedly and emphatically. But when the early revisionist writings appeared in the mid-1980s suggesting that Japan should be taken at its word and recognized as having deviated significantly from neo-classical free market principles, the message from Tokyo changed. Spurred in part by the

---

[10]Quoted in Pyle, *op. cit.*, p. 50.

[11]*Ibid.*, p. 54.

Ministry of Foreign Affairs and MITI, Japanese analysts and commentators filled the media with analyses purporting to prove that the Japanese economy is squarely within the neo-classical framework, and that the Japanese simply operate the neo-classical model more efficiently. Frictions are thus explained as a matter of poor Western performance, and American and European firms are thus urged to try harder.

One of the more reasoned of these commentaries came from Haruo Shimada of Keio University, who said of the revisionists, "Although their analysis is correct in some aspects, overall the revisionists' viewpoint lacks balance and is inappropriate, and the object of their policy is not constructive."[12] He went on to argue that Japan is well within the confines of the neo-classical model and that although some aspects of the Japanese system might be brought more into line with Western practices, many distinctively Japanese practices should be adopted in the West.

By the early 1990s, however, this wave had broken, and most Japanese analysts once again began to acknowledge Japanese uniqueness--including, ironically, some of the most vociferous critics of the revisionists. Former Foreign Minister and architect of the Japanese economic miracle Saburo Okita wrote, "There are many rooms in the house of capitalism. Japan may occupy some kinder, gentler middle ground between a centrally controlled economy and a laissez faire market driven economy. The Japanese experience is thus studied as one point of light."[13]

Moreover, the head of the cultural exchange Department of the Japanese Foreign Ministry, Kazuo Ogura, has noted that

> Both countries are democratic and have market economies. However, that is not the point. These two countries have taken an entirely different approach to these values at home and abroad. Many Japanese find the concepts behind personal liberty, democracy, and free market economics to be outlandish.[14]

Elsewhere, economist Iwao Nakatani has distinguished Japan's "network

---

[12]Haruo Shimada, "Is Japan's Economic System Different?" *Japan Close-Up,* September, 1991, pp. 5-8.

[13]Quoted in Chalmers Johnson, "History Restarted: Japanese-American Relations a the End of the Century," unpublished paper, 1992, p. 21.

[14]*Ibid.*

capitalism" from the Anglo-American version and Yukio Onuma of C. Itoh and Company has asserted that Japan is not a market economy in the Adam Smith mold."[15]

Most of these commentators are not well known in the United States. One exception is Sony Chairman Akio Morita. An outspoken critic of the revisionists, Morita recently shocked both Americans and Japanese with an article in a leading Japanese journal arguing that "We are approaching a point where continued competition by Japanese companies operating under a management philosophy alien to that of Europeans and Americans can no longer be tolerated."[16]

Morita's implicit embrace of the revisionist argument was then seconded by Gaishi Hiraiwa, the powerful head of Japan's big-business alliance, *Keidanren*: "In the eyes of Western business executives, Japanese businessmen and companies appear willing to sacrifice everything and think only of how to win when they compete. Shouldn't we relax somewhat and seek symbiosis with other countries?"[17]

In this light, the real question obviously is not whether the Japanese economy is considerably different from the neo-classical model, but rather, why so many American analysts keep denying this? Much of the answer is rooted in the Cold War. First, Americans wanted the occupation to be a success and defined success essentially as a Japan reformed along the lines of the American model. Thus there has always been a predisposition in the United States to see post-war Japan as a chip off the American block. Washington's efforts to keep Japan in the Western camp explain a great deal as well. For example, in 1964, with the Japanese economic miracle already proclaimed and with U.S. trade with Japan about to go into virtually permanent deficit, the State Department, aided by the U.S. Embassy in Tokyo, drafted a secret policy paper on the future of Japan. Edwin Reischauer was then the U.S. ambassador and he presumably continued to be concerned about Japan achieving a "satisfactory standard of living" because the paper strongly urged support of Japan's economic goals and recommended "firm Executive

---

[15]Quoted in Chalmers Johnson, "Japan in Search of a `Normal' Role," *Daedalus*, Fall, 1992, p. 8.

[16]Akio Morita, "'Nihon-kata keiei' ga abunai," *Bungei Shunju,* February 1992. Morita has also published a version of this article in English in the Summer 1992 issue of *Japan Echo.*

[17]T.R. Reid, "Japanese View US With New Negativity," *The Washington Post,* March 1, 1992.

Branch resistance of American industry demands for curtailment of Japanese imports."[18]

Such resistance could only be justified and maintained based on the assumption that U.S. and Japanese industry are competing under the same rules, and that U.S. industry should therefore not be aided if it loses out to Japanese competitors. Were it ever acknowledged that the Japanese were playing a different game, such a policy of support for Japanese economic goals could not be sustained. Thus for nearly 30 years, the U.S. government has assiduously perpetrated the notion that the Japanese economy is nothing more than a more efficient version of America's own.

The Japanese government clearly understood the situation and collaborated with U.S. policy. It was this collaboration that underlay official instigation and support of the virulent attack on the revisionists. As Peter Ennis noted in an article in *Tokyo Business Today* in January 1990:

> During the late 1980s, foreigners who made these same or similar observations [that is, the same as those of Japanese noted above] were stigmatized by the Japanese Ministry of Foreign Affairs as "revisionists". This was because the Ministry feared that accurate knowledge among foreigners about the structure of Japanese capitalism might lead to countermeasures against Japanese business activities, and it sought through propaganda and dirty tricks to prevent this from happening.[19]

The Japanese Model of Mixed Economy

No doubt a second reason is the relative paucity of book-length studies by Japanese authors available in English that seek not only to explain the distinctive features of the Japanese economic model, but that articulate the distinctive concepts and theories underlying them.

In this vein, *Beyond Capitalism* is a ground-breaking work. Moreover, its author, Dr. Eisuke Sakakibara, writes from an unusually authoritative vantage point. A graduate of the University of Tokyo and the University of Michigan, he has served in senior positions in the Japanese Ministry of Finance for most of the last decade and a half, currently holding the position of Deputy Director-General of the International Finance Bureau.

---

[18]Pyle, *op. cit.*, p. 34.

[19]Peter Ennis, *Tokyo Business Today,* January 1990, p. 30.

Sakakibara argues that over the past 60 years, Japan has developed a unique economic system--what he calls a non-capitalistic market economy. The key differences between the Japanese system and other market systems center on the structure of the private sector, the role of the public sector, and the relationships between the two. Of these, the structure of the private sector is most directly relevant to the debate between traditionalists and revisionists.

Unlike the private sectors of other advanced industrialized market economies, Sakakibara argues, the Japanese private sector has been practically bereft of true capitalists since the end of World War II. Because of the break-up of the *zaibatsu* ordered by the U.S. occupation authorities, Japanese companies were forced initially to rely for investment funds on U.S. aid plus a tightly regulated system of city banks, long-term credit banks, and public finance institutions. Even after many of the old *zaibatsu* reemerged as *keiretsu*, the restructuring of Japan's financial system left one critical change intact: Power within private businesses--and especially in Japan's largest companies--shifted from the "family capitalists" who founded them to the employees and other stakeholders. Writes Sakakibara, "It is in this sense that the post-war organization of large companies took on something of a more public hue. Specifically, managers were no longer working for the private interests of the family-capitalists, but for the common benefit of the organization's employees."

In other words, Japan's largest companies were no longer controlled by conventional stockholders. Instead, stakeholders were in charge. As the author notes, these managers "often combine an executive function with a supervisory function, somewhat akin to playing the twin roles of U.S. executive officers and corporate directors. Consequently, the Japanese companies put a greater stress than other companies on "striking some sort of balance between stockholder, employee, business partner, and consumer benefit, as well as local interest at times."

Eventually, the stakeholders themselves emerged as major sources or channels of finance, with the financial assets of Japanese non-financial institutions standing at levels unheard of elsewhere in the "capitalist" world. Intercorporate credit assumed unusual importance as well. The result has been the peculiarly Japanese phenomenon of interlocking shareholding, a corporate ownership pattern in which most of Japan's largest companies and banks own most of each other's stock, and which outsiders find almost impossible to penetrate. The percentage of shares held by individual stockholders stands today at only about one-third of the total, and has been declining steadily throughout the post-World War II period.

Backing up this system of "indirect finance" is a financial system proper that has been kept fragmented by government regulations, thus forcing financial institutions to offer tremendous incentives for depositors, and in turn fostering a high national savings rate. Consumer finance, by contrast, has occupied a trivial niche in the overall Japanese financial landscape.

To be sure, Sakakibara disputes some important aspects of some American revisionist arguments--principally the view that Japan's economic rise owes much to a relatively coherent economic plan drawn up by a reasonably unified bureaucracy and then followed by relatively cooperative Japanese companies. He also believes that some significant but limited Western-style practices have recently crept into the Japanese system, and that this trend will continue. Yet his broader conclusion unmistakably dovetails with that of the revisionists: "[I]t would be incorrect to assume that the Japanese system belongs to the same regime [as the American or European systems] just because it uses market mechanisms extensively and exists side by side with a democratic political system." And he adds that the "closedness" of the Japanese system that has so disturbed the rest of the world "cannot be opened unless the Japanese wish to change their regime from a non-capitalistic to a capitalistic economy."

As both revisionists and most traditionalists acknowledge, if such arguments are correct, America's Japan strategy would have to be completely overhauled. The Bush administration's resort to the Structural Impediments Initiative (SII) negotiations indicated that it had come to agree with several fundamental revisionist points: The Japanese system's structure and business practices make it inherently difficult to penetrate, while a top priority of Japanese government policy is promoting leadership by Japanese enterprises in key industries and technologies. With the U.S. system easy to penetrate by design, and with American leaders still cautious about industrial policy initiatives, American companies are left to compete in world markets on disadvantageous terms.

Like most other traditionalists, President Bush's response was to try to change Japan's system. But as Sakakibara argues, the Japanese system is not only extremely successful, it is a completely legitimate alternative to Western-style capitalism. His analysis supports the revisionists' fundamental criticism of the SII approach: Demands that Japan adopt a rough replica of the U.S. system can only breed resentment and resistance in Japan, further frustrate Americans, and poison the relationship.

This corrosive process will not be halted and reversed without intellectually honest analyses of the two economies and a willingness to admit that there are deep, systemic differences that cannot be defined out of existence, or removed by parochial, ethnocentric sloganeering. Eisuke Sakakibara has made a vitally important scholarly contribution to our understanding of the Japanese economy. *Beyond Capitalism* was published in Japan in 1990 as *The Japanese Model of a*

Mixed Economy. The Economic Strategy Institute is proud to bring this English-language edition to American and other readers, and hopes that it reaches the widest possible audience.

I. Prologue

In a recent article in *The New Yorker,* the noted economist and historian Robert Heilbroner handed down his final verdict: "Less than seventy-five years after it officially began, the contest between capitalism and socialism is over: capitalism has won."[20]

Indeed, the collapse of the Soviet Union and its empire, as well as the accelerating economic reforms in China, do seem to signal the end of socialism. Yet do these developments really imply a victory for capitalism? True, in most cases the marketplace has proved to be far more efficient than the "queues of the planned economy," business civilization has turned out to be "less worse" than state bureaucracy, and commercialism--however cheap and mindless--is much better than the ideological stifling of individual freedom.

What, however, is capitalism? Do we in the non-socialist world all live under capitalism? The author's answer to this question is an unequivocal no. Perhaps the United States offers us a relatively pure case of capitalism, but the European and Japanese models differ substantially from that of the United States, or from capitalism in any ideal form. Setting aside the European case, the author intends to argue here that Japan has developed a somewhat unique model of a mixed economy during the past sixty some-odd years (the Showa period) and established what might be called a non-capitalistic market economy with a pluralistic political regime.

Thus the real choice now facing the world seems to be not between capitalism or socialism, but between a capitalistic market economy or a non-capitalistic market economy. The non-capitalistic nature of the Japanese economy has recently

---

[20]Robert Heilbroner, "Reflections: The Triumph of Capitalism," *The New Yorker,* January 23, 1989.

become the source of various international frictions, including those involving merger and acquisition issues. A non-capitalistic regime has a built-in safety mechanism against classic capitalistic takeovers, as will be described later, and is basically closed to such attacks from outside. For many Americans and Europeans, this basic structural characteristic of the Japanese economy has become a symbol of Japanese "closedness." Indeed, there are many closed aspects that remain in the Japanese market that could be rectified with some effort, but this closedness cannot be opened unless the Japanese wish to change their regime from a non-capitalistic to a capitalistic economy.

Over the past ten years, the uniqueness of Japan's system has been debated at length by economists and business administration scholars. These specialists have developed a series of theories purporting to explain the Japanese economy, starting with the Japan Incorporated theory, and continuing with the Japan as Number One, and Japanese management theories. More recent ideas involve labor market theory, corporate theory, and "peoplism." For example, according to Keisuke Itami, professor of business administration at Hitotsubashi University, and others, the Japanese firm is regulated by humanism rather than capitalism, and is characterized by the sovereignty of the employee, the decentralization of information, and the internalization of the market.[21] Some, like Itami, believe that employee sovereignty supersedes both the pursuit of profit and shareholder gain. Others, like Kyoto University economist Masahiko Aoki,[22] characterize employee sovereignty as nothing more than one of several goals. Yet most analysts have correctly concluded that management for the stakeholders rather than management for the shareholders is an especially widespread practice in Japan.[23]

When we add the public sector to this non-capitalistic corporate sector, the result--at least on the surface--is a well organized but extremely competitive market economy with considerably egalitarian income distribution and high social mobility. Indeed, the system is quite internalized and, to the mind of individualistic Westerners, too well organized. To date, however, it has proved to be highly efficient and competitive.

---

[21]Keisuke Itami, *Jinpon Shugi Kigyo* (Chikuma Shobo, 1987).

[22]Masahiko Aoki, Kazuo Koike, and Iwao Nakatani, *Nihon Kigyo no Keizaigaku* (TBS Britannica, 1986).

[23]This concept of management for the stakeholders has also appeared in a pamphlet drawn up by the U.S. company, NCR, to promote its management policies. It is extremely interesting as an indication of the broad applicability of Japanese-style management. See George Melloan, "Business World," "NCR's Exley Manages for His 'Stakeholders'," *The Wall Street Journal,* June 16, 1987.

The author does not wish to compare the merits and demerits of the two systems here, but only to describe in full the structure of this non-capitalistic market economy as a legitimate socioeconomic regime that is not necessarily a unique outgrowth of Japan's unusual culture. The system is a legitimate heir of the revisionist moves towards a mixed economy taken after the Great Depression. It was primarily formed in the Showa period (1925-1989), reaching full maturity in the period of high growth following World War II.

II. A Mixed Economy à la Japonaise

Summary

The fundamental principle underlying the Japanese model of mixed economy is anthropocentricism, or what Keisuke Itami refers to as "peoplism." Peoplism is given concrete expression in the form of employee sovereignty within the corporation, and an emphasis on the independent, land-owning farmer within agriculture. This principle is clearly different from the ideological foundations of Western capitalism, and it would be incorrect to assume that the Japanese system belongs to the same regime just because it uses market mechanisms extensively and exists side by side with a democratic political system. Capitalistic elements have undeniably become more pronounced in the Japanese socioeconomic system over the past ten years or so, but they have not yet had any significant impact on this cardinal tenet of peoplism.

The most common ways of explaining the interactions between the Japanese public and corporate sectors have been the Marxists' traditional theory of state monopoly capitalism and the foreign Japanologists' Japan Incorporated theory. For all their differences, however, both schools of thought consider the public and corporate sectors in Japan to be monolithic--the Marxists emphasizing how the public sector is being subordinated to the corporate sector in one of the final stages of capitalistic development[24] and the Japanologists maintaining that the corporate sector is subordinated to the public sector within the framework of state corporatism. The strength of the argument for a monolithic Japan Incorporated as expressed in terms of harmony and consensus has waned. Yet political scientists T.J. Pempel of Cornell University and Keiichi Tsunekawa of Tokyo University,

---

[24]For example, Tsutomu Ohuchi, *Nihon Keizairon* (Todai Shuppankai, 1963).

for example, emphasize the leadership of the government bureaucracy within a corporate framework.[25] Political scientist Chalmers Johnson of the University of California at San Diego goes so far as to claim that "Japan's elite bureaucrats make almost all the major decisions, effectively draw up all legislation, oversee the national budget and are also the source of all major policies."[26]

The author's own experience within the government bureaucracy has conformed neither to the Marxist framework nor to the Johnson analysis. In actual fact, rivalries are extremely fierce within the public sector as well as between the public sector and its private sector counterparts. Squabbles between the Postal Savings agency and major private banks can surpass any in-fighting between the private banks alone, and the strongest enemy facing Daiei and Seibu, both private retailers who have to a large extent taken on and beaten the distribution system, is said to be the public livelihood cooperatives (*Seikyo*).

Elsewhere, the hold of the Ministry of Finance (MOF) and the Ministry of International Trade and Industry (MITI) over private companies is by no means great. Any influence they do wield is by and large indirect and based on a "mutual understanding" that is the product of a long-term process. Even in the energy field, where MITI's influence over private companies is somewhat stronger, its "long-time dream of creating a national oil champion continually producing and refining has failed to come about."[27] MOF also failed to strengthen regulations on disclosure and other areas of bank accountability at the time of the 1981 reform of the Bank Act, due to obdurate resistance by Mitsubishi Bank, the then-chairman bank of the National Bankers' Association.

What becomes apparent from these examples is the relative autonomy of the public and corporate sectors and the formation of a process of "mutual understanding" and continual negotiation that is based precisely on this premise of independence. I would like to make it clear, however, that the role of the public sector does not necessarily involve "political" intervention in the private sector by means of the budget or legislation aimed at some common public interest (e.g., economic growth or the fostering of industry). Rather its role is biased substantially towards securing the "economic" interests of its own projects. In

---

[25]T.J. Pempei and K. Tsunekawa, "Corporatism without Labor? The Japanese Anomaly," in P.C. Schmitter and G. Lembruch eds., *Trends toward Corporatist Intermediation* (Sage Publications, 1979).

[26]Johnson, *MITI and the Japanese Miracle, op. cit.*

[27]Richard J. Samuels, "Nihon ni Okeru Kokka no Business" (translated by Toshiya Kitayama), *Leviathan 2*, Spring 1988.

other words, most Japanese government intervention in the economy covers construction, public works, financial operations in the broad sense (including pensions), and, until very recently, transportation and communications works as well. Tokyo's pervasive intervention in agriculture is also well known. Yet in contrast to the United Kingdom and the most recent practices of other European countries, this type of direct market participation by the government does not occur in such key industries as energy and steel, and usually the key actor is not the central government but local government bodies or cooperatives and local companies closely linked to them. The grim reality, however, is that an important part of financing is managed by the central government, and that construction and public works as well as agriculture are managed by the direct participation of mainly local government bodies. Generalizations that ignore this key cornerstone of the Japanese politico-economic system are at best difficult.

In this light, significantly, U.S.-Japan economic friction is starting to focus on the domestic construction industry and the deregulation of agriculture. The system in these fields, where participation by the Japanese public sector is so prominent, has probably been targeted because it diverges so widely from the U.S. experience and has therefore caused a build-up of U.S. frustration. The pursuit of public works centering mainly on local government strongly binds local favoritism with political connections. Therefore it is extremely closed not only to Americans but to all the system's outsiders in general.

In any event, within the Japanese politico-economic system neither the public sector (which is based on finance, public works, and agriculture) nor the large corporate sector (which is dominated by manufacturing and some service industries) predominates. Rather, they co-exist in generally separate fields. It is this compartmentalized, dual system that forms one of the foundations of the Japanese-style mixed economy. Even though the public sector share is gradually falling, it still retains a finance and public works base significant enough to give concrete meaning to the aforementioned framework of continual negotiations and mutual understanding between the public and private sectors. More specifically, within the Japanese-style mixed economy, the large corporate sector and the public sector co-exist mainly in separate fields. They compete with considerable fierceness when they do overlap and mutually make related market and state choices within this compartmentalized competition.

This dual relationship between the large corporate groupings and the public sector becomes even more apparent when one reconsiders the history of Showa politics and economics. Japanese leftists and the U.S. occupation forces concurred in their assessment of the pre-war military and *zaibatsu* as monoliths. Moreover, this emphasis on the alleged lack of accountability on the part of the Japanese bureaucratic system reinforced the standard interpretation of pre-war Japan as a society in which party politics was crushed by the recklessness of these two villains, the military and the *zaibatsu*, which gave the weak-spirited liberals of the day no other choice but to follow their lead.

A frank look at the history of Showa uncolored by any ideological prejudice shows a slightly different picture. The following quote is taken from "An Ode to the Showa Restoration" ("Showa Ishin no Uta"), a poem that was very popular in the early Showa period, before World War II. It depicts the then prevailing public sentiment against the *zaibatsu* and the elder statesmen (*genro*): "The politicians boast of their power, but they don't concern themselves with the country. *Zaibatsu* possess enormous riches, but they don't have any sympathy for the poor."

Irrespective of how one appraises the "Showa Restoration," the critical point to be made is that out of the growing tenant-farmer strife, the ideology of physiocracy, triggered by the prolonged depression, gradually gathered strength from the early pre-war Showa period. This ideology finally culminated in a policy that might be termed the owner-farmer doctrine, which became the government's keystone policy. Against the backdrop of a popular backlash against the *zaibatsu*, this owner-farmer doctrine combined with the government's support for military industry and a new group of *zaibatsu* to produce a steady increase in the level of government intervention in agriculture and other key industries. In effect, the groundwork for land reform was gradually being laid as landlord powers were greatly emasculated by the 1924 Tenant Farmers Act, the 1938 Farm Land Adjustment Act, and the 1942 Food Control Act. The Land Lease and House Reform Act, which radically strengthened the rights of the lessee, was enacted in 1921 but applied only to urban areas. It was applied nationwide in 1941, thereby markedly curtailing landlord power in this area as well.

The slant of the military-public sector towards the new *zaibatsu* and their intervention in the industrial sector was further strengthened by parallel developments in the financial area--chiefly, the successive expansion of the Industrial Bank of Japan, the promulgation of the Provisional Funding Act (1937), and the 1942 enactment of the Bank of Japan Act.

Although initially the *zaibatsu* were bitterly opposed to these public sector moves--which were backed by public opinion and the military--some sort of mutual understanding was gradually reached with the government following the about-face by Mitsui's head director, Nariakira Ikeda. A system of cooperation with the government was consolidated. In the end, this arrangement came to be seen as cooperation with the military by the *zaibatsu*, but relations between the two forces during the early Showa period seem to have been anything but smooth--recall the assassination of Mitsui's chairman, Ikuma Dan, by ultra rightists.

As this process of cooperation was being consolidated, the large Japanese firms were gradually developing the foundations of what today is known as Japanese-style management. Although it is said that the power of the *zaibatsu* families was never as strong as that of corporate dynasties in the United States or Europe, the powers of the head clerk-president--men like Seihin Ikeda of Mitsubishi, Ichizo Kobayashi of Hankyu Electric Railway, Sanji Muto of Kenebo Textiles and Ginjiro Fujiwara of Oji Paper Manufacturing--grew during the Showa period, and the organization and institutionalization of *zaibatsu* management forged ahead quickly. As has also often been observed, it is about this same time that the concept of familial management gradually start to evolve into life-time employment and the seniority system. In other words, rather than a polarization of capital and labor, we find that the reduction of capitalist authority, the modernization of management organization, and the increase in employee sovereignty began to characterize the larger companies.

It is not difficult to conceive of this institutionalization of the *zaibatsu* and larger companies taking place in the context of antagonistic relations with an increasingly military-dominated public authority, as well as of a search for mutual understanding.

This drift toward establishing land-owning farmers and employee sovereignty within the Japanese politico-economic system was finally completed by the post-war reforms imposed by the United States. Although the 1946 land reform and the 1947 break-up of the *zaibatsu* were unprecedentedly thorough, the concept--or direction, if you like--of such policies had already been well established before World War II, with the then Ministry of Agriculture and Fishery playing a leading role in the area of land reform. To use a somewhat journalistic description, the economic system that was held up as the ideal of radical idealists on the Right was in actual fact introduced by U.S. officers at Occupation Headquarters (GHQ). The only difference was that democracy, not the Emperor system, had served as the catalyst. That such groups--so diametrically opposed from both a political and ideological perspective (ultra-nationalists on the Right versus New Dealers in the Government Section of GHQ)--would favor and put into place the same kind of economic system is one of history's ironies. It should be borne in mind, however, that both groups shared a strong animosity towards laissez-faire principles that was influenced mainly by the Great Depression of the 1930s.

In any event, the framework for the Japanese style of mixed economic was finally put together by the dissolution of the *zaibatsu* and land reform. Based on its underlying principle of anthropocentricity as expressed by the owner-farmer doctrine and employee sovereignty, it prepared itself for the high-growth period by operating under compartmentalized competition between the large corporate private sector and the public sector. Because the break-up of the *zaibatsu* eradicated virtually all of Japan's genuine capitalists, companies were left to rely on a regulated financial system consisting mainly of city banks, long-term credit banks, and public financial institutions for their plant and equipment investment. Management-centered corporate groups gradually formed through new, interlocking share holding and fund raising networks. The new companies emphasized technology developed through military production as well as imported from abroad, and were organized around the sort of professional managers, novelist Keita Genji dubbed "third-class executives." They pinpointed the export market as the area in which to concentrate their endeavors and gradually began to grow stronger.

Acting as guarantor or mediator, the state wielded some influence in this process, using finance, subsidies, and taxation as leverage. Nevertheless, corporations remained comparatively independent from the government, eventually playing at least in employee eyes the role of a semi-public autonomous body, or feudal domain, as opposed to a central government or *bakufu*. The most common illustration of this kind of independent corporate kingdom is the company town. Toyota, whose headquarters are located at Toyotatown 1-1, Toyota City, is a prime example, but most companies have something similar to either a greater or lesser extent.

Although the degree of independence can vary greatly, this relationship of relative independence and cooperation also exists between larger and smaller corporations. It has already been pointed out in many studies that it is misleading to interpret the relationship of large company and smaller subcontractor as merely one of control and subordination.

The rivalry and relative independence of companies from government and from each other has given rise to a decentralization of information and technology as well as a division of labor within Japanese corporate groupings. This is the source of what has been called excessive competition between Japanese corporations.

The public sector has still maintained its activities in such areas as construction, transport, communications, finance, and agriculture, all of which are based on the bureaucratic structure built up consecutively before World War II. During and after World War II, however, it underwent several fundamental changes.[28] One such change was the "democratization" of rural communities brought about by land reform, and the formation of agricultural cooperatives (*Nokyo*) to replace their pre-war counterparts, the *Nokai*. The *Nokyo* became a major regional force. Despite being subject to severe fiscal and budgetary controls, local authorities also grew into an important regional force in cooperation with cooperatives, their comparative independence from central government following the dismantling of the Ministry of Home Affairs. The role of politicians in this context also shifted gradually from the realm of diplomacy and other so-called high politics to low politics, or the implementation of public works, financial appropriations, and budgetary measures.[29] In a sense, Kakuei Tanaka was the very personification of the entrepreneurial politician, energetically implementing public sector construction and public works projects. As long as the great majority of Japanese companies stay based in large urban areas like Tokyo and Osaka, regional economic activity can only be encouraged by public sector projects that serve as lures to companies.

Moreover, budget appropriations from the central government are crucial to this process. The role of politicians in these circumstances is to comply with the wishes of local government and of the agricultural and other cooperatives within their constituencies, and to request appropriations from the central bureaucracy. They serve, in effect, as executive treasury officers stationed in Tokyo for their various regional institutions.

Of course, the role of politicians in a parliamentary and cabinet system also includes heading the executive branch of government, but there is no doubt that their real bread and butter is the treasury operations involving public projects in construction, civil engineering, agriculture, fisheries and forestry, transportation, telecommunications, and finance (including pensions).

It is in this type of setting that the central bureaucracy has come to play the role of mediator between regional and political interests, a role underpinned by its budgetary control. Rather than being coherently and intentionally planned, as claimed by some U.S. Japanologists, this mediation process is more in the nature of a passive, overall adjustment with the emphasis on balance.

---

[28]As a matter of form, agriculture of course is a private sector, but given the wide-ranging intervention, regulation, budgetary, and financial measures wielded by the Ministry of Agriculture and Fisheries, I would like to classify it here as part of the public sector.

[29]For an analysis of the Liberal Democratic Party see, for example, Seizaburo Sato and Tetsuhisa Matsuzaki, *Jiminto Seiken* (Chuo Koron, 1986).

To sum up briefly, the Japanese politico-economic system is characterized by a dual structure consisting of a large corporate sector and a public sector. The system blossomed during the high growth period of the 1960s and 1970s, and has the following main characteristics:

1. Anthropocentrism, as embodied in the owner-farmer doctrine and employee sovereignty. So-called egalitarianism and the puritanical work ethic can be considered corollaries of this underlying principle.

2. The co-existence of relatively independent organizations with competitive relationships; continual negotiation and mutual understanding between government and corporations, between corporations alone, between larger and smaller corporations, and between central and local government.

3. Politics and government administration centered mainly on public sector business, and a large corporate sector conducting operations on a fundamentally different plane.

The body of this study will look in greater detail at the Japanese style of a mixed economy, analyzing its past success and considering possible future problems. Assuming the establishment and perfection of a mixed economy à la Japonaise, the problems are likeliest to result from the rapidly changing circumstances of the last ten years, in which internationalization has played a major part, and from the widening gap between the Japanese mixed economy and this changing environment.

Calls for reform that lack a clear awareness of Japan's systemic realities have only led to a subservient Japanese pandering to frequent U.S. and European demands. The Japanese system of a mixed economy has enjoyed substantial success in the past, yet it is precisely because it is not sufficiently aware of its success that it has begun to stagnate and cannot carry out the reforms it needs. Moreover, it is its failure to nurture correctly the fruits of that success that is the basic cause of contemporary Japan's problems. Unless material wealth can successfully be turned into a sense of national identity and mental well-being, the Japanese will find themselves in a perpetual catch-up syndrome, always in a state of restlessness and mental hunger. It is about time that we take stock of our situation, live our lives at our own pace, and form our policies accordingly.

III. The Structure's Principle and Mechanism

Structure of the Large Corporate Sector

As discussed in the preceding section, the mixed economy à la Japonaise is a dual structure consisting of a large corporate sector and a public sector. In this section, let us briefly describe the large corporate sector, which shouldered the weight of Japan's high economic growth, by sifting through the work on this issue.

Looking at the issue schematically, although the internal structure of companies themselves and their management methods traditionally have been the subject of most analysis, inter-corporate relations (between groups or between large and small companies) or industrial structure is becoming another major focus. The first of these categories of inquiry falls into the field of Japanese management analyses or corporate theory, while the second comes more under the sway of industrial organization theory.

Regarding this first area, "Japanese specificity," in the form of the seniority system, life-time employment, and company unions, has been the subject of debate among Japanologists and labor economists. At least among economists, internal labor market theory has merged with contemporary corporate theory of a corporatist nature. In other words, by thinking of the market in abstract terms--i.e., as being internalized by implicit and long-term contracts--it has been possible to interpret the seniority system and life-time employment that seem to be so peculiarly Japanese as more general phenomena frequently witnessed in other industrial countries as well.

Undeniably, within the Japanese labor market, it is the permanent employees of large corporations who are the principal recipients of preferential treatment such as life-time employment and the seniority system. Yet they account for only some 30 percent of the total work force. Even in the United States, for example, a similar system exists for the core labor force of large corporations. It is therefore somewhat problematic to treat this practice as one unique to Japan. It is clear from empirical studies on quality circles and so on, however, that information is shared and a considerable degree of operational authority transferred all the way down the corporate ladder of the Japanese company. Unquestionably this information and power sharing heightens the sense of oneness and boosts employee loyalty.

Yet even as information and operational authority are decentralized in Japan, other functions are more centralized than in other countries' systems. For example, the Japanese head office has a strong tendency to conduct corporate management through the control of personnel and budget. (U.S. companies, by contrast, tend to manage their organizations through the concentration of information.) As will be discussed later, this preoccupation with budgets and personnel is extremely pronounced among senior Japanese government bureaucrats as well. As a result, the top echelons in Japan often have an insufficient grasp of the nuts-and-bolts of their operations. Because information as well as analysis functions are so decentralized in this "bottom-up" decision-making, the result is often vertical organization and an inability to respond swiftly to sudden external changes. At the same time, such organizations excel in terms of strengthening flexible on-the-scene response, and of encouraging a sense of unity within the organization.

It is natural not just for Japanese companies but for companies in general to aim at more than merely maximizing profits for stockholders. Management everywhere involves some sort of balance between stockholder, employee, business partner, and consumer benefit, as well as local interest at the time. The question here is whether Japanese companies and companies in other industrial countries hold different relative priorities. Even if a corporate management model is suitable as a general framework, as Aoki asserts, the character of a company can change greatly depending on where the priority is placed. It is in this sense that Itami's emphasis on employee sovereignty and his description of Japanese corporate management concepts as peoplism become credible.

It was argued in the previous section that, along with land reform, the break-up of the *zaibatsu* was critical to creating the Japanese-style mixed economy. The effective eradication of Japan's pool of capitalists by this reform had a substantial impact on the shape of Japanese firms thereafter. It is true that managers played a larger role even in the pre-war *zaibatsu* organizations than in the United States or Europe. Yet the position of managers was not at all ambiguous, and it would be difficult to claim that it deviated to any large degree from the domain of the family's head clerks. The fall of the families after the dissolution of the *zaibatsu*, however, changed the manager from the head clerk for the family to the figure at the top of an employee organization. It is in this sense that the post-war organization of large companies took on something of a more public hue. Specifically, managers were no longer working for the private interests of the family/capitalists, but for the common benefit of the organization's employees. Even if the corporate organization was private when compared to the larger public body of the state, it took on a public nature vis-a-vis the individual interests of each company employee. Managers acted as village heads in their para-community of the company; it is in this sense that their role had a considerable public dimension.

Japanese managers often combine an executive function with a supervisory function, somewhat akin to playing the twin roles of U.S. executive officers and corporate directors. This has led to frequent comments on the difficulty of introducing external checks on the Japanese manager. In fact, however, this hybrid would only seem natural in the Japanese economic system, devoid as it is of a pool of capitalists.

It is not the board of directors, then, that delegates power to a manager in Japan, but the employees. Consequently it is only natural for the selection of a manager to be a long, drawn-out internal process. Responsibility to other stakeholders apart from employees--such as stockholders, business partners, and consumers--is always determined on the basis of market transactions (irrespective of whether they are internal or not). Yet responsibility towards employees is decided mainly through the organization. In this way, the rule of employee sovereignty within the Japanese form would seem to be fairly well established.

Although it may seem rash to say that there are no capitalists in Japan or that the Japanese economic system is not capitalistic, such statements are nevertheless sufficiently suitable expressions of a rough, general proposition. Moreover, in order to come to terms with the Japanese politico-economic system, they strike at the heart of the matter. What, then, are the Japanese stockholders? Is there really no final control exercised by stockholders? And how do Japanese economic mechanisms fill in this capitalistic vacuum?

Table I illustrates average ownership of stocks for six major corporate groups and non-affiliated major corporations between 1974 and 1982. As can be clearly seen from this table, whether a firm belongs to a corporate grouping or not, some 30 to 40 percent of its stocks are held by financial institutions, with a further 20 to 30 percent being held by non-financial institutions. In other words, some 60 to 70 percent of outstanding stocks are held by financial institutions and related companies inside or outside a corporate group. Individual stockholders account for only 30 to 40 percent of the total. Moreover, the ratio of shares held by individual stockholders has been following a downward curve in the post-war period.

TABLE 1

CORPORATE STOCKHOLDING BY GROUP (1974-1982, AVERAGE PERCENT)

Group	Financial Institutions	Non-Financial Institutions	Individuals	Non-Residents/ Others	Total
Mitsui	37.0	29.3	30.9	2.8	100.0
Mitsubishi	39.6	22.7	34.7	3.0	100.0
Sumitomo	34.8	32.0	30.8	2.4	100.0
Fuji	37.1	23.4	36.0	3.5	100.0
DKB	41.2	21.9	33.5	3.4	100.0
Sanwa	40.2	22.1	35.3	2.4	100.0
Subcontractors	17.1	55.1	23.6	4.2	100.0
Non-affiliated	37.2	19.3	40.0	3.5	100.0

N.B.   From Nakatani (see Footnote 30).

In the case of a typical firm, first on the list of stockholders come life insurance companies, trust banks, and/or city banks, with holdings of three to four percent of total shares each. For example, the backbone of the Mitsubishi Group, Mitsubishi Heavy Industry's main stockholders, are Mitsubishi Trust and Banking, the Mitsubishi Bank, Meiji Life Insurance, and Sumitomo Trust and Banking. The main stockholders for Hitachi, Ltd., core of the non-*zaibatsu* Hitachi group, are Mitsubishi Trust and Banking, Nippon Life Insurance, Mitsui Trust and Banking, Toyo Trust and Banking, and the Industrial Bank of Japan. What is of greatest interest here is that even in companies like Matsushita Electric and Sony, where the owner-management pattern is comparatively strong, the holdings of the Matsushita family and the Morita family's share of Reikei Company (its de facto holding company) only amount to 2.6 percent and 7.8 percent, respectively. In other words, even in firms that started out as simple owner companies, the owner has become less prominent as the organization grows, and a more general form of interlocking stockholdings seems to become a rule.

Generally speaking, as long as the company in question maintains good relations with those companies accounting for this 60 to 70 percent of its stock (in many cases, they are often business partners, and stockholding is reciprocal), such stocks work for the management. In many cases, therefore, hostile takeovers are effectively impossible and, at least in the case of major corporations, it is extremely difficult to purchase enough stock to acquire management rights.

In other words, for many managers, concern about stockholders involves maintaining good relations with related financial institutions and major companies, as well as realizing long-term profits mainly in the form of capital gains. The stockholders' annual general meeting, as a result, is reduced to nothing more than a skeletal ceremony. Many critics, particularly in the area of commercial law, argue that the result is a disregard of stockholder sovereignty. Yet this argument is irrationally based on legal formalism; it fails to acknowledge the real and distinctive nature of the Japanese economic system. To the Japanese joint-stock company, the issue of equity is akin to an issue of low-interest corporate bonds (or non-voting preferential stock), and is considerably removed from the concept of company ownership. Although Japanese corporate managers do have the responsibility of distributing suitable profits to stockholders as one group of stakeholders in the company, the weight of that responsibility is considerably lighter than that towards their employees. Economist Iwao Nakatami of Hitosubashi University, for one, has analyzed this interlocking stockholding as follows:

> In many cases, reciprocal equity holdings are extremely widespread, stockholders at the top of the list being firms within the same corporate grouping and financial institutions. As this takes place on a reciprocal basis, the policies chosen by a firm often reflect the interests of the group as a whole and even go against those of the ordinary stockholder (of the company concerned). This kind of inter group finance and diversification or internalization of the capital market through interlocking stockholding isolates group companies from competition in the capital market. As a result of this isolation from the capital market, group companies are able to select their own policies free from market competition. As mentioned above, no corporate takeover by stockholders will occur even if the corporate management concerned does not maximize the company's market value but pursues the interests of the company's direct participants. This is because the major stockholders are insiders protecting the interests of current management. Even if, for example, current stock prices are markedly low and capital cannot be raised from the market for a necessary investment project, the city banks and other financial institutions within the group will meet the fund demand of the company concerned.[30]

Here Nakatani is only concerned with the firm within a corporate grouping, but his analysis can be applied virtually as it stands to non-affiliated companies as well.

As one of the main characteristics of peoplist firms, Itami cites market internalization as well as employee sovereignty and power and information sharing. Indeed, the internalization of the capital market and the labor market is a very pronounced feature of Japanese industrial structure. Although this internalization

---

[30]Iwao Nakatani, "The Economic Role of Financial Corporate Grouping" in M. Aoki, ed., *The Economic Analysis of the Japanese Firm* (North Holland, 1984).

of the capital market has undergone rapid changes in the 1980s, it has dominated the structure of Japanese money and capital markets throughout the Showa period, especially the post-war period, and shaped the regime of what may be called Japanese financial intermediation.

As has often been pointed out, the background to this internalization of the money and capital markets is the existence of a financial system overwhelmingly dominated by indirect finance. Table 2 depicts recent outstanding personal financial assets in the United States and Japan. The large share of banks, small- and medium-sized financial institutions and the Post Office in Japan shows up in the size of demand and time deposits.

TABLE 2

COMPOSITION OF PERSONAL FINANCIAL ASSET BALANCE IN JAPAN AND THE UNITED STATES (PERCENT)

	United States			Japan		
	1976 ($1 B)	1981 ($1 B)	1987 ($1 B)	1976 (¥ 1 T)	1981 (¥ 1 T)	1987 (¥ 1T)
Cash, current deposits (including ordinary deposits)	4.6	4.2	4.4	16.0	12.0	9.5
Term, savings deposits	22.0	18.8	18.5	48.0	51.4	45.3
Money market fund	0.1	2.6	2.7	--	--	--
Credit market assets[1]	8.9	8.6	10.6	7.0	7.7	5.5
Investment trust	1.2	0.6	3.9	1.6	1.6	4.7
Stocks	17.9	14.7	14.9	9.0	7.1	9.9
Insurance[2]	4.4	3.2	2.5	12.1	13.4	17.5
Trust fund	--	--	--	6.1	6.2	6.3
Pension	12.8	14.0	19.6	--	--	--
Other[3]	28.1	33.1	22.9	0.3	0.6	1.3
Total	3,959.2	7,122.1	11,747.1	209.3	388.1	703.1

Sources: *Koshasai yoran* (Compendium of government and corporate bonds), 1988.

Notes: 1. Government securities, state and local government securities, corporate bonds, foreign bonds, mortgage bonds, open market papers, etc.
2. Life insurance only for the United States.
3. Equity (U.S.) in incorporated businesses.

Further, unlike in West Germany, Japanese indirect finance is not controlled by major private sector banks. That is, almost 40 percent of the overall aggregate of total and financial debentures in March, 1988 was accounted for by small- and medium-sized financial institutions such as agricultural cooperatives, fishing cooperatives, postal savings, *sogo* banks (mutual cooperative banks), credit unions, and workers' credit unions. Table 3 shows that his trend was already pronounced in the early Showa period and gathered further speed after World War II.

TABLE 3

PROPORTION OF DEPOSITS AND FINANCIAL BONDS OF VARIOUS FINANCIAL INSTITUTIONS IN AGGREGATE DEPOSITS AND BANK DEBENTURES (PERCENT)

	1910	1920	1930	1940	1950	1960	1970	1979	1987
Commercial banks and savings banks[1]	72.8	70.3	47.4	46.4	57.4	49.9	41.9	35.0	35.7
Five major banks[2]	12.7	14.4	14.7	15.5	38.3	32.8	26.2	20.5	21.4
Provincial banks[3]	60.1	55.9	32.7	30.8	19.1	17.1	15.6	14.5	14.3
Long-term credit banks[4]	14.4	14.9	13.0	10.4	8.9	5.7	6.0	5.7	5.4
Trust institutions	--	--	7.6	8.1	2.7	10.1	9.6	11.7	11.9
Mutual banks, shinkin banks, credit associations, including cooperatives[5]	0.3	2.2	7.1	13.5	17.4	19.5	25.5	25.1	22.7
Life insurance companies	3.8	4.4	6.6	5.6	2.0	4.1	6.0	5.7	9.3
Post Office	8.6	8.2	16.3	16.0	11.5	10.7	11.0	16.8	15.0
Aggregate deposits and bank debentures[6]	2,010	10,916	21,680	62,816	1,617	17,020	97,658	377,994	758,739

Source: For the pre-war period: H. Patrick, "Senkanki nikeru Nihon kinyu seido no seisei," in *Senkaiki no Nihon keizai bunseki*, T. Nakamura, ed., (Tokyo: Yamakawa Shuppansha, 1981); for the post-war period, Bank of Japan, *Keizai tokei nenpo* (annual report on economic statistics for each year).

Notes:
1. Figures are the totals of the commercial and savings banks. There were no savings banks after the war.
2. Figures are for Daiichi, Sumitomo, Yasuda, Mitsui, and Mitsubishi before the war. The post-war figures are for metropolitan banks.
3. The 1940 figure includes Sanwa, which was created as a result of the 1933 merger.
4. The pre-war figures are for specialty banks. (*tokushu ginko*).
5. Including the Shoko Chukin Bank (Commerce-Industry Cooperative Central Fund) and the Norinchukin Bank (Agriculture-Forestry Central Fund).
6. Pre-war figures in million yen, postwar in billion yen.

It is well known that the internalization of the labor market became pronounced from the early Showa period and continued throughout that era. Yet little attention was paid to the fact that the Japanese indirect financing system--its main elements being the city and regional banks alongside such smaller financial institutions as the Post Office and agricultural or fishing cooperatives--was also more or less completed at the same time. These two trends should clearly be considered as having progressed and supplemented each other simultaneously, with both representing elements of the process of building up the Japanese style of a mixed economic system.

The author has previously argued that Japanese indirect financing methods are not "backward" compared to those of other industrial countries, as many have charged. Instead, they represent an effective system with a certain rationality of its own.[31] In other words, it was precisely this regime of Japanese indirect finance that had supported the Japanese model of a mixed economy. The development of the Japanese indirect finance regime--minus ideological prejudice concerning its "backwardness"--can be summed up briefly as follows:

1. Although the trend was interrupted by the Second World War, the financial assets of Japanese non-financial institutions have risen intermittently in the Showa period, reaching in the 1980s an extremely high level as compared to the United States. As is well known, during the high-growth period the corporate sector acted as the counterpart to this accumulation, and switched later to the public and overseas sector.

2. As mentioned earlier, this extremely far-ranging financial intermediation was backed up not only by city banks, regional banks, and other major financial institutions, but also by more plebeian financial institutions like the postal savings system, and the various coops and credit unions.

3. Inter-corporate credit such as commercial bills has reached an extremely high level in comparison to other industrial countries. This development is intimately related to the fact that the major firm within a corporate group acts as a sort of financial institution for the smaller, related firms. As will be discussed later, the relationship between large and smaller firms is not one of controller and subordinate even when

---

[31]E. Sakakibara, R. Feldman, and Y. Harada, *The Japanese Financial System in Comparative Perspective* (Joint Economic Committee, U.S. Congress, March 12, 1982).

strong ownership bonds through stockholding are present. Rather, the relationship is of a comparatively autonomous nature. Yet indirect control through finance and personnel (for the latter, when ownership relations exist via equity) is considerably stronger.

4. The largest of the government's roles in finance consisted of its own financial intermediation. Competitive relations in the fund raising arena--among the postal savings scheme, the agricultural cooperatives, and private financial institutions in particular--made it impossible for the major financial institutions to exercise oligopolistic control. The result was fierce competition within the government's regulated framework (i.e., in non-price areas).

This competition, coupled with the sheer size of the postal savings system and the agricultural coops, is probably one of the reasons behind the high savings rate in Japan, a middle-class society where income distribution is relatively equitable.

After all, most economic theory holds that the more unfair the distribution of income, the higher the savings rate will be. Yet in Showa Japan, especially post-war Japan, income in the lowest bracket was well above the survival level. Thus the low-income bracket saved almost the same portion of its income as the high-income bracket. Further, the ambitions of the lower-middle class in a classless society acted as a strong incentive to save. In short, saving in Japan, with its lack of a capitalist class, was high in all income brackets--which are predominantly middle-class.

5. Until very recently, consumer finance was comparatively trivial. Japan's mixed economic system has always stressed the so-called supply side, and a large demand surplus existed in the financial markets until the 1970s. An additional factor on the investment side-- as opposed to the fund raising side--is that, except for the Housing Loan Corporation, the government created no financial institutions that catered to the consumer. Reflecting post-war growth needs, financial intermediation by the government on the funds investment side was confined to the supply side. The Exim Bank and Japan Development Bank (JDB) catered to big business, the Medium- to Small-Enterprise Finance Corporation to smaller business, and the Development Finance Corporations for Hokkaido, Northeastern Japan, and Okinawa to promoting regional development.

Consequently, the Japanese regime of indirect finance is characterized by fierce competition and rivalry between the private and public sector financial institutions on the fund raising side, and by a compartmentalized division of business on the investment side. The global tide of financial deregulation in the 1970s quickly removed some of these partitions and brought dramatic change to the Japanese financial system. Just how the Japanese system of indirect finance and public financial institutions responds will probably be crucial for the future evolution of its mixed economy.

The relationship of this point to the whole will be dealt with in the final chapter, so let us now consider the second characteristic of the Japanese industrial structure--the relationship between large and small firms. This point was often argued at one stage after the war in the form of the so-called two-tier structure theory. The view that smaller firms were subordinated to large companies and made up an oppressed sector was made as a kind of common sense argument based on wage differentials and productivity differentials. But is this view truly valid? For example, even wage differentials between large and small companies are not out of line after adjusting for the quality of labor and other conditions, especially for core workers. Nor can rates of profit margin for smaller companies be dismissed as low.

Instead, a more accurate idea of the structure of Japan's mixed economic system can be ascertained by looking empirically at how relations are maintained between larger and smaller firms, and what sort of role these firms play vis-a-vis each other.

First, consider the oft-mentioned fact that in Japan smaller companies account for a much higher share of both the workforce and the number of businesses than in other industrial countries. Small firms with fewer than 1,000 employees accounted for some 85.7 percent of total Japanese employees in 1984, whereas the corresponding figure in the United States was 74.9 percent in 1982 and in the United Kingdom 65.1 percent in 1982. This disparity is largely attributable to the fact that the subcontracting system (where first-, second-, and even third-string subcontractors can be found), which is hinged on contracting companies, creates a division of labor that does not exist in either the United States or Europe. Toyota's 60,000 employees, for example, only amount to a tiny 9 percent of GM's 700,000, but Toyota has 600 first-string subcontractors. Each subcontractor operates under an extremely sophisticated division of labor, delivering a specific number of parts at a specific time in the so-called just-in-time (*kanban*) system. Each subcontractor also generally has business dealings with second-string subcontractors or hundreds of other suppliers. Thus several thousand companies can contribute to the manufacture of one automobile through a division-of-labor network. This system would be inconceivable for manufacturers in other industrial countries where major corporations are directly involved themselves in the manufacturing process more or less from start to finish.

As already mentioned, developments in major corporate organization in the Showa period after the break-up of the *zaibatsu* radically altered the nature of managers. Rather than acting principally as entrepreneurs, managers began to stress balanced management. Smaller firms, however, have featured a much higher proportion of owner-managers, with many firms thus retaining a strong entrepreneurial nature. In larger firms, so-called salarymen-managers account for the great majority of managers and organization is considerably bureaucratic.

For reference purposes only, Chart 1 illustrates figures on business starts and closures according to corporate size. As can be seen, the smaller the firm, the higher the number of both, which attests to the significant contribution made by small-firm mobility and maneuverability to change and renewal in the industrial structure.

CHART 1

BUSINESS STARTS AND CLOSURES

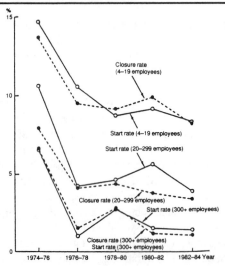

Figure 1: Changes in Business Start and Closure Rate by Size of Firm (Annual average, manufacturing)

Source: Chusho kigyo hakusho (The medium and small business white paper), 1986. Data are from the Ministry of International Trade and Industry, *Kogyo tokei hyo* (Census of manufacturers).

Notes: Start rate = [(Number of establishments started during applicable period)/(Number of establishments at beginning of same period)] x (1/2) x 100

Closure rate = [(Number of establishments closed during applicable period)/(Number of establishments at beginning of same period)] x (1/2) x 100

Chart 2 details the profession of the founders of small firms before start-up, and shows that small firms themselves are a significant breeding ground for small-firm founders. More than 70 percent of them from 1965 on started as managers or employees of small firms.

CHART 2

PREVIOUS PROFESSION OF SMALL FIRM FOUNDERS

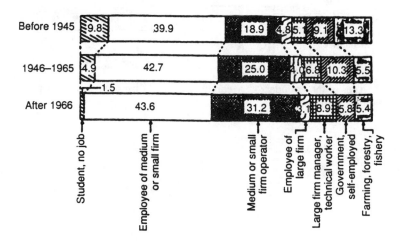

As Chart 3 shows, most of the founders are between 26 and 35 years of age, and this age group accounts for more than 50 percent of founders who were once small-firm employees. In order words, small firms form the most active and flexible sector of the Japanese economy, adapting in an extremely dynamic way to business starts, closures, and changes in scale, as well as acting as their own entrepreneurial seed bed.

CHART 3

AGE OF SMALL FIRM FOUNDERS

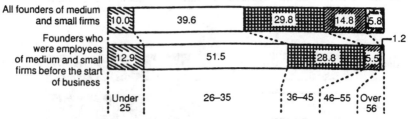

Figure 3: Ages of the Founders of Medium and Small Firms at the Start of Business (Manufacturing, %)

As already mentioned, apart from the case of wholly or nearly wholly-owned subsidiaries, the relationship between larger and smaller firms, or between contracting company and subcontractor, is one of relative independence. Any control of the subcontractor is more likely to take place via business transactions or finance. Between 1945 and 1965, when finance was comparatively tight, the extent of indirect control through finance in its broad sense (which would include bill discounting) was probably fairly high. Yet as corporate fund raising became easier in the 1970s and 1980s, when financial conditions eased, control through financial means gradually declined.

The 1987 White Paper on Small- and Medium-sized Business analyzes changes in subcontracting organization structure caused by recent changes in the economic environment. Several of the instances cited pointed to the relatively independent pattern of subcontracting firms and these examples are worth quoting at length:

1. **Top-class Subcontractor Diversifies Contracting Firms.**
Company A (65 employees) is engaged in parts manufacture and pressing for information processing and communications equipment, and was established in 1957 as a subcontractor for the manufacture of computer cabinets for a major electrical manufacturer. In recent years, it has upgraded its technology and factory automation through an exchange with a foreign company and has expanded its operations to include information processing and computer systems, software development, and biotechnology R&D. In its relations with its contracting companies, it has established its own management format by responding carefully to user needs through a small-lot, multi-type production system. It has now developed into a subcontractor dealing with some 10 companies, mainly major electrical manufacturers.

2. **Top-class Subcontractor Jointly Develops New Products with Contracting Companies.**
Company B (56 employees) started out as a subcontractor for four major construction companies when founded in 1976, and was commissioned to design and manufacture engineering- and construction-related measuring instruments. Its priority from 1978 was the development of new products and it is involved in joint research projects with each of its contracting companies, successfully taking out a patent for a product jointly developed with one of its contracting companies in 1985 (a measuring instrument that shows the degree of variation in underground pipes). The subjects of its joint research projects are decided upon in consultation with its contracting companies; trial manufacture and experiments are carried out by Company B while its contracting companies provide research fund support and advice on products for trial manufacture.

3. **The Development and Marketing of New Products Through Exchange with Other Companies in Different Fields.**
Company C (175 employees) is involved in presses, sheet metal, and the assembly of microwave oven doors as a subcontractor for an electrical manufacturer. It is very eager to develop new products and joined a prefectural research group in 1978, using its plating and press know-how successfully to develop equipment for mixed oil and water combustion with another member of the research group. It has its own sales network in conjunction with the prefectural environmental pollution division and the boiler association, orders being received from hotels, the dry cleaning industry, and dyers.

4. **The Development and Marketing of New Products Through Exchange with Other Companies in Different Fields.**

Company D (52 employees) was originally a subcontractor for the manufacture of automobile springs, but developed a highly sophisticated, computerized wire bender, which it has marketed through another company. Although Company D had the technology for wire bending, it was not strong in the area of computers or electrical machinery, yet it was able to produce this product in cooperation with two companies in the same city for exchange between different industries. The metal patents formerly used are no longer needed, thereby facilitating trial manufacture and small-lot, multi-type production. (pp. 126-135).

To sum up this brief sketch of major corporations in the Japanese private sector:

1. The core of the Japanese private sector is formed by major corporations whose interlocking share holdings keep them independent from capital. Each firm is managed along fairly decentralized lines through the wide dissemination of information and operational responsibility. Yet there is a strong tendency towards centralized control of personnel and finance and, as such, these companies are organized as "bottom-up" bureaucratic systems.

2. The internalization of both labor and financial markets formed the backdrop to the organization of a personnel and financial system in the major corporations. By internalizing the money and capital markets, the so-called Japanese model of an indirect financial system probably supported the control exercised by major firms through personnel and finance.

3. Each major firm has business dealings with an extremely large number of smaller firms in the form of subcontracting, but these relations are not characterized by direct control and subordination. They are either founded on concrete transactions or take more indirect forms--through financial support and so on. The relative independence of subcontractors is considerable and has increased in recent years. Compared to the relatively bureaucratic flavor and the bottom-up organization of major companies, smaller firms are more capitalistic, have a strong top-down tendency in their operations, and are both more mobile and dynamic. These contrasting methods of management and organization in major and smaller firms in the Japanese private sector--as well as their competitive but complementary relations--are characteristic features of the Japanese mixed economic system. Here, as well as in the relations of rivalry and cooperation that exist between the public and private sectors, is the major source of the Japanese system's dynamism.

Structure of the Public Sector

As stated earlier, to this point, analyses of the Japanese public sector by both Marxists and Japanologists alike have stressed public sector intervention by means of regulations, budget policy, fiscal investments in and loans to the major private corporations, or the mutual involvement of these two parties. Although so-called state-monopoly capitalism and the Japan Incorporated argument express different views on the structure of authority, they agree that the fundamental structure of the Japanese public sector consists of extremely close relations between the state and the private sector, and of coordinated moves between these two players.

The previous section pointed out, by contrast, that the basic relationship between the public sector and the major private corporate sector was one of *comparative independence*, and that in areas where public and private sectors overlapped, fierce competitive relations existed. In other words, the public sector and the private sector--and specifically the major corporations--are engaged in "compartmentalized" competition in basically *independent* forms. It is in this context that a constant process of negotiation is used to shape mutual understanding, with both market and state choices being made in a reciprocally related manner.

In this section, an international comparison of the structure of Japan's government expenditure will be used to show that Japanese public spending heavily emphasizes public works and social insurance (especially pensions). At the same time, although social security is indeed the largest item on the public expenditure side, final government consumption (for items such as medicine and welfare) is much lower than in other industrial countries. Thus the conclusion that Japan has started down the road toward a European-style welfare state is not accurate. Of the ¥10 trillion appropriated in the fiscal 1989 budget for social security, for example, 61 percent, or ¥6.6142 trillion, is for social insurance and more than half of that sum is pension-related.

Bearing in mind the fact that pension and insurance operations are very much state financial operations, and that postal savings, pensions, and postal life insurance account for a large share of the Fiscal Investment and Loan Program (FILP is the annual program of asset management of the trust fund of the Ministry of Finance's Financial Bureau), the Japanese public sector slants largely towards *finance as an enterprise*, along with public works. Certain Japanologists and some Marxists have dealt extensively with MITI-centered industrial policy as the key contribution by the public sector, and this policy is often viewed as the model for all government-private sector relations. In the end, however, this view only produces the state-monopoly capitalism or Japan Incorporated argument, or a variant thereon, and has substantially misled analysts of the Japanese public sector.

Undisputedly, there was in the 1940s-1950s a move to support military and other key industries through a combination of regulations based on industrial law, taxation and fiscal investments, and loans, as well as government expenditures. Yet these policies were only one aspect of the process of compartmentalized competition and mutual understanding between the public and private sectors that evolved throughout the Showa period. I believe it is untenable to view this framework as the fundamental structure of the public sector. Regulations have retreated substantially since the deregulation of trade in 1960, and the composition of the fiscal investments and loans directed into key industries at this time has also changed dramatically.

That is to say, there was no consistent targeting or grand design of industrial policy by the government. More likely, the government selected key industries as investment and loan recipients because of their vigorous, long-term demand for funds and their relative creditworthiness, responding more less passively to market demands rather than creating them. This process was of course not solely dictated by economic principles. As will be shown later, it also inevitably involved political considerations as well. Yet rather than these considerations consisting of political pressure from MITI acting as a policy headquarters, it would be more accurate to think of them in terms of so-called pork-barrel politics by the industries concerned. In any event, it would be wrong to believe that consistent targeting or a grand design of industrial policy by the government as a whole existed in Japan. MITI policies and administration have merely existed on the same level as the policies of other ministries aimed at aiding construction, transport, agriculture, and fisheries, or supporting the public welfare system.

As a matter of fact, Japanese public sector activities primarily revolve around public works and financial operations. In order to clarify this point, an international comparison of final government expenditure and an analysis of the Fiscal Investment and Loan Program will be used on a macro level. Irrigation and drainage works in the public works area, and postal savings in the financial area, will be examined on a micro level.

Let us first look at Table 4, which expresses general government's final consumption and fixed-capital formation in terms of the GDP using National Account statistics.[32] Looking at the sum total of final consumption and

---

[32]*National Account Detailed Tables, Volume II 1973-85* (OECD Department of Economics and Statistics, 1987).

investment, the Japanese figure of 14.54 percent falls far below the 20 percent or so found in the other major economies. Yet although Japan would appear to have the smallest government in this sense, a closer look at the data shows that it is only final government consumption that is small (some 10 percent, compared to 20 percent or so of the other industrial countries). Government fixed-capital formation is two or three times higher than in the other major economies.

TABLE 4

RATIO TO GDP OF GOVERNMENT FINAL CONSUMPTION AND FIXED-CAPITAL FORMATION (PERCENT)

	Japan (1985)	United States (1985)	United Kingdom (1985)	Germany (1984)	France (1982)
Government final consumption	9.73	18.31	21.13	19.96	16.20
Central government	2.37	8.69	12.89	3.76	11.35
Local Governments	7.28	9.63	8.00	9.74^2	3.82
	$(7.37)^1$	$(2.83)^1$	$(6.65)^1$	$(3.51)^1$	$(3.63)^1$
Government fixed capital formation	4.81	1.60	1.89	2.29	3.06
Central government	0.79	0.36	0.90	0.31	0.63
Local government	4.06	1.24	0.99	1.82	2.19
Total	14.54	19.91	23.02	22.25	19.28
Central government	3.16	9.05	13.79	4.07	11.98
Local governments	11.34	10.87	8.99	11.56	5.99

Source: OECD Department of Economics and Statistics (1987).

Notes: 1. Central government's transfer to local governments.
           2. Sum of state or provincial government and local government.

In a planned economy, the GDP ratio of government expenditure usually is raised by large government fixed-capital formation. In Japan, however, the GDP ratio of government expenditure is kept low despite an extremely high level of government fixed-capital formation. Also critical is the fact that nearly 80 percent of central and local government expenditure takes place at the local government level. This ratio has also been higher than that of the former West Germany (74 percent) and the United States (54.6 percent), and much higher than that of France and other countries with large central government expenditure. As is well known, a large proportion of Japanese taxes make their way to regions as local grants and subsidies, with transfers from the central to local governments in 1985 amounting to 7.37 percent of GDP--much higher than the corresponding figure for other major economies.

TABLE 5

RATIO OF GOVERNMENT FINAL CONSUMPTION TO GDP (1985, PERCENT)

	Japan	United States	United Kingdom	Germany	France
Government final consumption	9.73	18.31	21.13	19.96	16.20
Salary and wage component	7.74	10.88	--	--	11.37
(Government final consumption-- salary and wages)	1.99	7.43	--	--	4.85
General service	2.57	1.16	1.08	2.04	2.10
Defense	0.94	6.57	5.12	2.79	3.49
Public safety	*	1.15	1.64	1.55	0.91
Education	3.58	4.41	4.77	3.98	5.31
Medical care	0.41	0.84	3.92	5.94	0.49
Welfare	0.53	0.61	1.45	2.03	1.20
Housing	0.57	0.39	0.69	0.29	0.91
Culture-religion	0.23	0.18	0.47	0.46	0.60
Economy	0.98	2.33	1.31	0.89	1.16

Source: See Table 4.

* included in general service

Table 5 gives a category-by-category breakdown of final government consumption. The much higher final government consumption witnessed in other major economies can be attributed to their greater defense, medical, welfare, and education costs. The discrepancy in defense spending--in which Japan only manages a tiny one-seventh to one-third the level of the United States and Europe--sticks out most prominently and is a major source of U.S. and British criticism of Japan as a free rider. Medical and social welfare spending is also much higher in Europe, with its strong leanings towards the welfare state. Generally speaking, spending on education is also higher in the West than in Japan.

Figures for the share of final government consumption accounted for by wages and salaries tell a similar story. The GDP ratio of wages and salaries subtracted from final government consumption is a minimal 2 percent in Japan, 7.4 percent in the United States, and 4.9 percent in France. Although the ratio of wages and salaries is itself low, final government consumption in Japan is also very low after this figure has been subtracted, representing only 40 percent of government fixed-capital formation.

Next, Table 6 illustrates the share of total fixed-capital formation accounted for by government fixed-capital formation.

TABLE 6

SHARE OF GENERAL FIXED-CAPITAL FORMATION (PERCENT)

	1975	1980	1985
Japan			
Ratio to GDP of aggregate fixed-capital formation	32.45	31.57	27.72
Ratio to GDP of government fixed-capital formation	5.29	6.11	4.81
(including government enterprise)	(9.05)	(9.53)	(6.83)
[Government fixed-capital formation (including	27.88	30.19	24.64
government enterprise)]/[Aggregate fixed-capital formation]			
United States			
Ratio to GDP of aggregate fixed-capital formation	17.19	19.13	18.64
Ratio to GDP of government fixed-capital formation	2.12	1.76	1.60
(including government enterprise)	(2.98)	(2.57)	(2.17)
[Government fixed-capital formation (including	17.32	13.41	11.62
government enterprise)]/[Aggregate fixed-capital formation]			
United Kingdom			
Ratio to GDP of aggregate fixed-capital formation	19.86	18.18	17.15
Ratio to GDP of government fixed-capital formation	4.82	2.39	1.89
(including government enterprise)	(8.42)	(5.28)	(3.52)
[Government fixed-capital formation (including	42.38	29.04	20.52
government enterprise)]/[Aggregate fixed-capital formation]			
Germany			
Ratio to GDP of aggregate fixed-capital formation	20.39	22.71	19.53
Ratio to GDP of government fixed-capital formation	3.87	3.59	2.29
[Government fixed-capital formation (including	18.98	15.81	11.73
government enterprise)]/[Aggregate fixed-capital formation]			
France			
Ratio to GDP of aggregate fixed-capital formation	23.27	21.90	18.90
Ratio to GDP of government fixed-capital formation	3.56	2.85	2.88
[Government fixed-capital formation (including	15.30	13.01	15.23
government enterprise)]/[Aggregate fixed-capital formation]			

Source: See Table 5.

Note: For Germany and France, no data are available for government enterprise.

As is well known, the 30 percent GDP ratio of total Japanese fixed-capital formation is approximately 10 percentage points higher than the corresponding figure in other major countries, and the 25 to 30 percent share of government fixed-capital formation in total fixed-capital formation is also far higher than elsewhere. The inclusion of public corporations under general government expenditures would raise the GDP ratio for fixed-capital formation to 7 percent even in 1985, far above the 2 percent recorded in the United States or the United Kingdom's 3.5 percent. These shares are by no means negligible despite their gradual reduction owing to privatization and/or cutbacks in expenditure. In particular, the government and public corporation share of total fixed-capital formation in the United Kingdom has been more than halved--from 40 percent in 1975, when a considerable portion of key industries was run by the public sector, to less than 20 percent in 1985 under the Thatcher government.

Table 7 illustrates the same discrepancies on a government expenditure basis. The transfers balance ratio in Japan accounts for 30 to 50 percent of general government expenditure, a share similar to final government consumption, and a figure worth watching in a country where it has been climbing yearly. This increase is caused by the rise in social insurance expenditure, including pensions and medical insurance, generated by an aging population. In fact, social insurance's 28 percent share of expenditure in 1985 already surpassed the corresponding figures in the United States, United Kingdom, and West Germany.

TABLE 7

SHARE OF GENERAL GOVERNMENT EXPENDITURE ITEMS

	1975	1980	1985
Japan			
Total expenditure (billion yen)	39,875	77,080	102,992
Final consumption	37.34	30.57	29.85
(Salary-wage component)	(31.96)	(25.14)	(23.74)
Interest payment	4.50	9.87	13.90
Subsidies	5.53	4.66	3.53
Other transfer balance	30.24	32.91	35.36
(Social insurance component)	(22.04)	(24.54)	(28.08)
(Social security component)	(6.76)	(6.81)	(5.78)
Fixed-capital formation	19.66	19.05	14.76
Land purchase	2.72	3.11	2.60
(Fixed-capital formation + land purchase)	(22.38)	(22.16)	(17.36)
United States			
Total expenditure (million dollars)	554,840	919,464	1,457,593
Final consumption	53.03	51.52	49.58
(Salary-wage component)	(34.25)	(31.98)	(29.47)
Interest payment	6.91	9.22	13.64
Subsidies	0.92	1.17	1.57
Other transfer balance	32.68	32.70	30.70
(Social insurance component)	(19.08)	(19.61)	(19.45)
(Social security component)	(10.28)	(9.71)	(7.96)
Fixed-capital formation	6.04	5.14	4.34
Land purchase	0.43	0.26	0.18
(Fixed-capital formation + land purchase)	(6.47)	(5.40)	(4.52)

(Continued)

TABLE 7

SHARE OF GENERAL GOVERNMENT EXPENDITURE ITEMS

	1975	1980	1985
United Kingdom			
Total expenditure (million pounds)	48,996	103,678	164,107
Final consumption	47.22	47.22	45.12
Interest payment	10.57	12.52	12.62
Subsidies	7.52	5.54	4.74
Other transfer balance	23.51	28.64	33.01
(Social insurance component)	(13.12)	(14.00)	(13.58)
(Social security component)	(6.35)	(9.25)	(12.79)
Fixed-capital formation	10.19	5.30	4.03
Land purchase	--	--	--
France			
Total expenditure (million francs)	622,858	1,273,409	2,398,587
Final consumption	33.58	33.13	31.16
(Salary-wage component)	(23.71)	(22.53)	(--)
Interest payment	2.98	3.49	5.31
Subsidies	4.60	4.15	4.39
Other transfer balance	50.26	52.94	53.56
(Social insurance component)	(37.50)	(41.17)	(41.62)
(Social security component)	(5.60)	(5.06)	(4.78)
Fixed-capital formation	8.31	6.22	5.51
Land purchase	0.26	0.08	0.06
(Fixed-capital formation + land purchase)	(8.57)	(6.30)	(5.57)
Germany			
Total expenditure (million marks)	484,610	687,500	839,900
Final consumption	43.34	43.31	43.54
Interest payment	2.68	4.00	6.45
Subsidies	4.21	4.44	4.40
Other transfer balance	41.58	40.53	40.59
(Social insurance component)	(25.92)	(25.37)	(25.61)
(Social security component)	(7.21)	(6.29)	(5.84)
Fixed-capital formation	7.72	7.32	4.79
Land purchase	0.48	0.40	0.22
(Fixed-capital formation + land purchase)	(8.20)	(7.72)	(5.01)

Source: See Table 6.

To summarize:

1. Final expenditure by the Japanese government is markedly smaller than that in other major economies because of lower expenditures on defense, medical care, and education.

2. The Japanese government's fixed-capital formation is far greater than that of the other major economies. Particularly when coupled with public corporations, its GDP ratio comes to 7 percent and accounts for one quarter of total fixed-capital formation in Japan. This is more than double the U.S. or German share and is higher even than the percentage in the United Kingdom, where public corporations have gradually been privatized. Moreover, in contrast to the United Kingdom, where public sector fixed-capital formation is almost evenly split between government proper and public corporations, the government proper accounts for more than twice the share of public corporations in Japan.

3. Nearly 80 percent of final government expenditure in Japan takes place at the local government level. The regional share of government fixed-capital formation stands at 85 percent. This ratio has been far higher than that of the former West Germany or the United States. Moreover, much of this local final expenditure has been covered by a transfer of treasury resources from the central government in the form of grants and subsidies.

4. The transfers balance, which covers social insurance and social welfare, has already reached U.S. and U.K. levels. And although it is still small by European standards, its share is gradually climbing. The 28 percent share accounted for by social insurance (1985) in particular is far higher than the corresponding U.S. figure, and has been even higher than the former West Germany's 26 percent (as of 1980).

The above expenditure structure of Japanese central and local government demonstrates a pronounced slant towards government fixed-capital formation and social insurance. But consider the activity of another key government policy instrument--the Fiscal Investment and Loan Program. Table 8 shows the FILP for fiscal 1988 and 1989, of which investment and loans to public works institutions in the fiscal 1989 budget accounted for ¥4.1831 trillion. This figure represents 16 percent of the ¥26.3405 trillion sub-total excluding the financial investment portion. Bear in mind, however, that virtually all of the finance for regional public bodies, as well as a portion of the funding for financial intermediaries, ultimately will find its way into public works or related work.

TABLE 8

OVERVIEW OF FISCAL YEAR 1989 FISCAL INVESTMENT AND FINANCING PLAN
(IN 100 MILLION YEN AND PERCENT)

Agency	1988 initial plan		1989 plan	
General fiscal investment				
1. Public works orgns.	41,217	(1.3)	41,831	(1.5)
Japan Road Corp.	18,972	(6.9)	19,160	(1.0)
Tokyo Metropolitan Region Highway Corp.	2,565	(21.9)	2,684	(4.6)
Hanshin Region Highway Corp.	2,191	(23.0)	2,449	(11.8)
Honshu-Shikoku Connecting Bridge Corp.	1,121	(-49.9)	1,293	(15.3)
Housing-Urban Improvement Corp.	8,664	(0.1)	8,685	(0.2)
2. Housing Loan Corp.	47,071	(13.0)	50,933	(8.2)
3. Other funds and banks	73,574	(8.3)	78,800	(7.1)
People's Finance Corp.	18,838	(0.0)	20,100	(6.7)
Small Business Finance Corp.	18,030	(3.8)	18,460	(2.4)
Agriculture, Forestry and Fisheries Finance Corp.	4,720	(6.7)	4,400	(-6.8)
Japan Finance Corp. for Municipal Enterprise	11,910	(17.8)	12,100	(1.6)
Japan Development Bank	8,940	(7.3)	10,500	(17.4)
Import-Export Bank of Japan	6,800	(50.4)	8,520	(25.3)
4. Other public program orgns.	44,128	(11.3)	49,741	(12.7)
Pension Welfare Program Orgn.	11,780	(5.5)	14,657	(24.4)
Japan Railroad Construction Corp.	1,518	(-38.0)	1,322	(-12.9)
Japan National Railways Settlement Orgn.	13,810	(12.4)	10,425	(-24.5)
Overseas Economic Cooperation Fund	4,910	(105.9)	5,680	(15.7)
Total (general fiscal investment excluding local governments)	205,990	(8.5)	221,305	(7.4)
5. Local government public program orgns.	47,450	(0.0)	42,100	(-11.3)
Total	253,440	(6.8)	263,405	(3.9)
Trust Fund Bureau Programs				
Postal Savings Special Account	25,000	(25.0)	30,000	(20.0)
Pension Welfare Program Orgn.	12,700	(27.0)	15,300	(20.5)
Postal Insurance and Postal Annuity Welfare Program Orgn.	5,000	(42.9)	14,000	(180.0)
Total	42,700	(27.5)	59,300	(38.9)
Grand Total	296,140	(9.4)	322,705	(9.0)

Source: See Table 7.

Notes: The rate of increase over the preceding year is shown in parentheses. In addition to the above, national bonds underwritten in the amount of 2.3 trillion yen (3.5 trillion yen in Fiscal 1988).

Therefore, almost 50 percent of both the direct and indirect investment and loans of the FILP--excluding the financial investment portion--will be accounted for by public works. Moreover, funds to the Housing Loan Corporation and other finance corporations amount to ¥12.9733 trillion, or 49 percent of general investment and loans. Since financial investment is clearly also a financial activity, adding in funds involved in FILP financial activities yields a total of ¥18.9033 trillion, or some 59 percent of the program's total funds.

Given that FILP is a gross investment flow of more than five-year maturity, however, it is difficult to say that its programs always represent an accurate picture of government investment activity at any particular moment. It is for this reason that the details of the Trust Fund balance sheets are given in Tables 9 and 10. On a fiscal 1987 settlement basis, Trust Fund Department assets totaled ¥197 trillion. Of the ¥140 trillion remaining after the exclusion of government bonds, financial debentures, cash, and other resources, a considerable portion is public-works-related loans. This fact would seem to confirm the overwhelming share also accounted for by civil engineering and the public works on the investment and loan side of the Japanese public sector.

TABLE 9

BALANCE SHEET OF THE TRUST FUND BUREAU (IN MILLION YEN)

	FY 1985 year end	1986	1987
Assets			
Long-term national bond	39,519,912	47,983,821	53,673,124
Short-term national bond	92,962	38,622	61,122
General account and special account	16,218,445	22,370,370	24,947,119
Semigovernment organizations	62,460,989	59,310,758	54,347,758
Local public body	23,204,785	25,110,706	27,092,681
Special corporations	22,671,431	23,541,632	33,709,173
Bank debentures	2,055,026	2,169,712	2,570,140
Other	844,090	824,396	902,513
Cash	414	468	286
Total	167,068,054	181,350,485	197,303,916
Debt			
Postal savings and postal transfer deposits	101,324,291	103,871,519	116,828,752
Postal life insurance and postal pension transfer deposits	2,575,125	3,050,128	3,763,264
Worker insurance transfer deposits	50,304,376	55,099,767	59,684,122
National pension transfer deposits	2,492,862	3,072,077	3,638,226
Other transfer deposits	10,260,593	11,136,282	13,262,184
Other	110,777	120,712	127,378
Total	167,068,054	181,350,485	197,303,916

Source: See Table 8

TABLE 10

ASSET STATEMENT OF THE TRUST FUND BUREAU (IN MILLION YEN)

	FY 1986 year end	1987	Change
Long-term national bond	47,983,821	53,673,124	5,689,303
Short-term national bond	38,622	61,122	22,500
General account and special account	22,370,370	24,947,119	2,576,749
General account	10,887,665	10,887,665	0
Revenue-sharing tax and transfer tax allocation special account	6,144,355	5,913,935	-230,420
Designated national property maintenance special account	10,000	16,792	6,792
Coal-oil substitution measure special account	--	12,600	12,600
National school special account	411,688	438,266	26,578
Worker insurance special account	1,378,423	1,389,481	11,058
National hospital special account	539,183	560,685	21,502
National forestry projects special account	1,514,006	1,698,037	184,031
National land improvement project special account	781,049	823,011	104,962
Foreign trade insurance special account	164,100	219,500	55,400
Airport maintenance special account	25,700	56,300	30,600
Postal service special account	85,300	91,500	6,200
Postal savings special account	--	2,013,600	2,013,600
Road maintenance special account	346,000	649,700	303,700
Flood control special account	6,156	3,770	-2,386
Urban development fund finance special account	139,745	172,277	32,532
Semigovernment orgns.	59,310,758	54,347,758	-4,963,000
Japan Railway Corp.	7,390,172	--	-7,390,172
Japan Telegraph & Telephone Corp.	77,231	47,836	-29,395
People's Finance Corp.	4,577,120	4,618,100	40,980
Housing Loan Corp.	26,756,063	29,411,355	2,655,292
Agriculture, Forestry, and Fisheries Finance Corp.	4,941,002	4,961,587	20,585
Small Business Finance Corp.	3,494,979	3,358,951	-136,028
Hokkaido, Tohoku Development Finance Corp.	116,160	141,026	24,866
Environmental Sanitation Business Corp.	579,780	560,840	-18,940
Okinawa Development Finance Corp.	697,657	714,148	16,491
Japan Development Bank	6,546,261	6,725,905	179,644
Import-Export Bank of Japan	4,134,333	3,808,010	-326,323
Local Public Orgns.	25,110,706	27,092,681	1,981,975
Special Corps.	23,451,632	33,709,173	10,167,541
Housing-Urban Development Corp.	7,748,436	7,537,277	-277,159
Japan Highway Public Corp.	2,368,627	2,428,907	60,280
Forest Development Corp.	181,265	195,737	14,472

(Continued)

TABLE 10

ASSET STATEMENT OF THE TRUST FUND BUREAU (IN MILLION YEN)

	FY 1986 year end	1987	Change
Maritime Credit Corp.	138,974	153,632	14,658
Tokyo Expressway Public Corp.	186,678	224,755	38,077
Water Resource Development Public Corp.	608,145	673,283	65,138
Hanshin Superhighway Corp.	139,343	171,758	32,415
Japan Railroad Construction Corp.	1,616,896	457,843	-1,159,053
New Tokyo International Airport Corp.	68,523	59,469	-9,054
Petroleum Corp.	58,935	47,336	-11,599
Tokyo Bay-Yokohama Port Pier Corp.	6,583	3,731	-2,852
Kobe Port-Osaka Port Pier Corp.	12,667	9,247	-3,420
Honshu-Shikoku Connecting Bridge Corp.	193,358	215,196	21,838
Agricultural Land Developing Public Corp.	167,959	175,223	7,264
Regional Development Corp.	202,070	206,003	3,933
Labor Welfare Projects Orgn.	89,407	80,407	-9,000
Employment Promotion Projects Orgn.	100,080	93,246	-6834
Pension Welfare Service Public Orgn.	5,614,186	7,386	1,772,061
Metal Mining Agency of Japan	23,306	22,171	-1,135
Public Nuisance Prevention Corp.	372,250	·331,965	-40,285
Small Business Promotion Corp.	73,963	60,788	-13,175
Social Welfare-Medical Care Projects Corp.	792,409	732,771	-59,638
Japan Sewage Projects Corp.	4,080	14,720	10,640
Sinkansen Railway Maintenance System	--	2,663,869	2,663,869
Tokyo Rapid Transit Authority	222,209	220,353	-1,856
Nippon Ikueikai	40,518	71,718	31,200
Overseas Economic Cooperation Fund	2,176,950	2,469,183	292,233
Japan Private School Promotion Foundation	333,815	322,102	-11,713
Japan National Railway Settlement Program Orgn.	--	6,598,258	6,598,258
Eastern Japan Passenger Railroad Corp.	--	37,596	37,596
Tokai Passenger Railroad Corp.	--	13,712	13,712
Western Japan Passenger Railroad Corp.	--	28,695	28,695
Japan Freight Railroad Corp.	--	1,975	1,975
Bank debentures	2,169,712	2,570,140	400,428
Other	824,396	902,513	78,117
Cash	468	286	182
Total	181,350,485	197,303,916	15,953,431

Source: See Table 9.

Elsewhere, the fact that ¥54 trillion--or 39 percent of the ¥140 trillion in total investment and loans--is lent to government-related financial institutions amply illustrates the large role played by the public sector in the financial arena. Moreover, this figure only pertains to the asset side. As already mentioned, if postal savings, pensions, and postal insurance from the liability side are added in, it becomes crystal clear that finance is just as important a mainstay of the Japanese public sector's entrepreneurial activity as public works.

Let us now analyze in detail the structure of public works and financial operations, citing some specific examples. Tables 11 and 12 look at public works in terms of statistics on domestic construction investment. Of the ¥58.6 trillion in total construction investment forecast for fiscal 1987, the government accounts for 40 percent. Of the ¥23.99 trillion in civil engineering works covered therein, the share of government investment climbs to a phenomenal 82 percent. Moreover, 34 percent of the bodies commissioning public works on a fiscal 1986 basis were prefectures and 31 percent were towns and villages. Local government thus accounted for an overwhelming share of total government construction investment. The share of the central government was a small 11 percent. The item-by-item share of public works in order of increasing importance is roads, sewerage/parks, agriculture/fisheries/forestry, education/hospitals, and flood control works.

TABLE 11

ESTIMATED CONSTRUCTION INVESTMENT (IN 100 MILLION YEN)

Item	FY 1978	FY 1980	FY 1983	FY 1986	FY 1987
Total	387,986	494,753	475,988	529,200	586,000
Building	231,284	292,189	274,693	318,200	346,100
Residential housing	140,007	160,170	147,846	172,000	193,000
Government	8,781	8,847	9,102	7,900	8,800
Private sector	131,226	151,323	138,744	164,000	184,900
Nonresidential housing	91,277	132,019	126,847	146,200	152,400
Government	26,772	39,202	32,924	28,300	29,300
Private sector	64,505	92,817	93,923	117,900	123,200
Mining and manufacturing	12,031	31,640	19,958		
Other	52,474	71,177	73,965		
Road and bridge construction	156,702	202,564	201,295	211,000	239,900
Public works	82,778	112,974	124,994	143,200	172,800
Other than public works	73,924	89,590	76,301	67,800	67,000
Total:					
Government	150,513	196,192	198,994	203,200	241,800
Private	297,473	298,561	276,994	326,000	354,230
Building					
Government	35,553	48,049	42,026	36,200	38,000
Private	196,731	244,140	232,667	282,000	308,000
Road and Bridge					
Government	114,960	148,143	156,968	167,000	193,800
Private	41,742	54,421	44,327	44,100	46,100

Source:　Ministry of Construction, Bureau of Construction Economics, ed., *kensetsu tokei yoran* (An overview of construction statistics), 1988.

Note:　The figures for 1976 and 1977 are rounded to the nearest 10 billion yen. Therefore the sum for each item does not necessarily add up to value for total.

TABLE 12

ASSESSED VALUES OF PUBLIC WORKS PROJECTS AT THE TIME OF PROJECT START (FISCAL YEAR 1986, MILLION YEN)

Contracting organization	Total cases	Landslide and flood control	Agriculture, forestry, and fisheries	Highways	Seaports and airports	Sewerage and parks	Education and hospitals
Total	11,062,734	1,062,842	1,177,739	2,769,699	407,986	1,318,277	1,084,927
National government	1,239,074	254,914	112,774	393,766	100,000	8,461	110,138
Semigovernment corps.	722,664	12,689	28,421	447,139	3,416	12,912	3,035
Public project corps.	125,957	0	0	0	0	601,252	31,001
Government enterprises	548,456	16,635	17,701	0	102,912	0	5,157
Prefectures	3,765,629	682,573	654,693	1,041,122	153,303	278,819	238,981
Municipalities	3,400,952	88,888	289,158	802,401	32,029	77,088	671,124
Local govt. enterprises	832,432	5,393	0	39,857	8,444	162,094	8,196
Other	427,569	1,751	74,992	45,412	7,882	20,650	17,295

Contracting organization	Housing, hostels	Government buildings and other	Disaster reconstruction	Land creation	Railways	Postal service	Electrical power and natural gas	Consumer and industrial waterworks	Maintenance and repair
Total	652,924	770,240	552,712	217,580	283,821	15,240	48,130	418,206	312,411
National government	50,093	122,195	59,195	2,024	0	0	0	0	25,514
Semigovernment corps.	139,122	32,780	1,582	27,176	108	0	0	4,022	10,263
Public project corps.	15,336	14,622	0	1,329	0	0	0	0	3,418
Government enterprises	8,333	31,068	8,053	0	223,199	15,240	28,069	0	92,000
Prefectures	163,094	167,159	320,552	27,357	0	0	0	0	37,976
Municipalities	165,296	275,472	130,683	84,181	0	0	0	0	86,631
Local government enterprises	15,623	53,558	892	21,658	60,514	0	20,061	394,490	41,651
Other	96,029	73,386	1,755	53,856	0	0	0	19,694	14,868

(Continued)

TABLE 12

ASSESSED VALUES OF PUBLIC WORKS PROJECTS AT THE TIME OF PROJECT START (FISCAL YEAR 1986, MILLION YEN)

By Contracting Organization

Year	Total number	National government	Semigovernment corporations and public project corporations	Government enterprises	Perfectures	Muncipalities	Local government enterprises	Other
1977	9,755,507	1,049,123	831,425	1,439,784	2,736,181	2,734,436	620,582	387,976
1978	10,189,008	1,071,467	741,521	1,567,210	2,945,154	2,808,770	632,813	423,074
1979	10,756,632	1,176,409	898,403	1,509,422	3,043,174	2,847,427	823,968	457,430
1980	11,439,796	1,279,012	1,013,339	1,418,248	3,182,782	3,180,059	882,040	484,101
1981	11,459,796	1,200,973	948,192	1,338,148	3,314,030	3,249,209	846,743	563,500
1982	11,698,642	1,264,977	961,539	1,275,959	3,489,183	3,274,050	874,182	558,752
1983	10,966,015	1,218,129	991,598	1,142,359	3,293,805	2,931,783	877,486	510,854
1984	10,293,987	975,685	811,404	906,729	3,234,519	3,181,263	762,579	421,809
1985	10,999,990	1,172,433	890,865	800,053	3,526,768	3,328,817	848,134	432,919
1986	11,062,734	1,239,074	818,621	548,456	3,765,629	3,400,952	832,432	427,569

Source: See Table 11.

Irrigation/drainage projects under the Special Account for National Land Improvement are good examples of agriculture/fisheries/forestry works, which account for almost 10 percent of all public works. Examining them enables us to outline the interaction between the national government, prefectures, and beneficiaries (cities, towns, villages, land improvement cooperatives, and individuals). As shown in Table 13 and Chart 4, in addition to government-run projects, the central government provides subsidies to prefectural and collective works.

TABLE 13

MECHANISM OF IRRIGATION AND DRAINAGE PROJECTS
(SELECTION CRITERIA AND SUBSIDY RATE BY SPONSOR AND BY REGION)

		National Government	Prefecture	Organization
Selection Criteria	Honoshu Shikoku Kyushu	over 3,000 ha	200 ha	over 20 ha
	Hokkaido	1,000	200	20
	Okinawa	1,000	100	20
Subsidy rate	Special Acct	50%	50%	50%
	General Acct.	60%		
Hokkaido	Rice field	70%	55%	50%
	Field	85%	55%	55%
			Soil Conservation 50	Shelter 50
Small islands		--	55	50
Okinawa		85	80	80
Amami		--	70	60

Source: See Table 12.

Note: Even within Honshu, Shikoku, and Kyushu, the selection criteria and subsidy rates are relaxed in special areas such as sparsely populated areas.

CHART 4

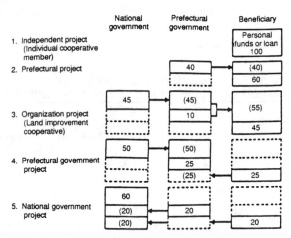

Figure 4: Mechanism of the Irrigation and Drainage Burden Bearing

Depending upon the specifics of the project, the central government, prefecture, or land improvement cooperative is responsible for the respective funding burdens--except in the case of genuinely individual works. As land improvement coops often overlap cities, towns, and villages, the land improvement cooperative burden is borne according to the respective standing of the city, town village, and coop members. Land improvement measures can be moved by 15 or more coop members if they have the approval of two-thirds of their members. Because the motion then goes to the Minister of Agriculture and Forestry via the prefectural governor for its suitability to be determined, even the individual works of a coop member, for example, cannot be carried out without prefectural and national approval. In short, although it is the cooperative that determines needs and moves motions at the bottom of the ladder, the actual works themselves are closely controlled by the national government and the prefecture. Of course, the bodies that carry out these works are often the prefecture, city, town, village, or land improvement cooperatives; the central government confines itself to the supervisory role of fund supplier except in the case of certain national works.

Unfortunately, space does not permit a detailed explanation of how the state, local government, cooperatives, and individuals interact in all public works, and interaction does vary considerably according to the type of project involved. Yet the following generalizations can probably be made about public works as a whole:

1. In the process of implementing public works, the state plays an overseeing role as fund supplier rather than acting as the direct instigator. Even in the area of roads, where the share of the state and public corporations is comparatively large, it still only accounts for 30 percent. This state role is extremely important when subsidies and other direct funding are combined with the previously mentioned indirect fund supply of investments and loans.

2. Although the prefecture often instigates work programs directly, it also plays a role similar to that of the state as fund supplier.

3. Although cities, towns, and villages can have strong presences as instigators, the coops (land improvement coops, agricultural coops, fisheries coops, forestry coops, the chamber of commerce, etc.) as well as small, local companies are linked inseparably. Works therefore often take the shape of joint regional projects and have fairly close associations with the local private sector.

Next let us look at an example of the government's financial activities, the postal savings system. The Post Office and private financial institutions have battled throughout the postwar period over the question of postal savings. Further, this issue has often been politicized by the involvement of many politicians on the Post Office side, and very few objective analyses have been made of either the postal savings system or public sector finance in general. In particular, arguments about public finance costs, including taxation issues, and the impact of the rivalry on the market have often been emotional and most likely based on inaccurate data. Let us instead try to present as objective an image as possible.

Table 14 compares the balance of postal savings with the balance of bank-held deposits (commercial banks) since Meiji.

TABLE 14

POSTAL SAVINGS BALANCE AND BANK (COMMERCIAL BANK) DEPOSIT BALANCE

	Postal savings balance[1] (A)	Growth rate[5]	Bank deposit balance[2] (B)	Growth rate[5]	A/B (%)	Postal savings interest[3] (%)	Bank Interest[4] (%)
	(10,000 yen)						
1877	21.2	253.3	n.a.	--	n.a.	5.00	7.97
1882	151	60.6	n.a.	--	n.a.		7.62
1887	1,821	17.8	n.a.	--	n.a.		4.70
1892	2,283	6.9	32.52 M yen	57.9	70.2		4.39
1897	2,616	8.1	27.74	46.4	12.6		5.89
1902	3,046	8.9	536.70	19.2	5.7		6.93
1907	9,770	19.2	944.00	-8.6	10.3		5.41
1912	20,124	4.5	1,357.00	14.8	14.8		5.30
1917	32,836	36.3	2,256.00	14.6	14.6		4.27
1922	90,116	1.8	6,444.00	10.6	14.0	5.70	
1926	125,354	7.4	9,178.00	5.2	13.7		
1930	249,715	13.4	8,738.00	-6.0	28.6	4.20	
1935	323,296	5.5	9,950.00	5.4	32.5		
1940	791,502	28.6	24,671.00	23.6	32.1		
1945	4,715,182	55.2	102,349.00	67.9	46.1		
1950	15,470,000	26.8	928,600.00	30.5	16.7	3.50	
1955	.5383 T yen	18.3	3.5801 T yen	22.1	15.0		
1960	1.1231	13.8	8.4995	19.6	13.2		
1965	2.7025	21.2	19.6449	15.5	13.8		
1970	7.7439	22.6	38.9248	14.4	19.9	5.75	5.75
1975	24.5626	26.4	87.398	14.6	28.2	8.00	8.00
1980	61.9498	19.3	147.366	9.0	42.1	7.25	7.25
1985	102.9979	8.9	225.6053	8.9	45.4	5.25	5.25

1. Postal savings balance does not include postal loss and profit savings, the fiscal year-end figures, or figures compiled by the Postal Savings Agency.
2. (Commercial banks); For 1877-1945, from Bank of Japan, *Honpo shuyo keizai tokei* (Economic Statistics of Japan); after 1945, from Bank of Japan, *Keizai tokei nenpo* (Annual Report on Economic Statistics). Figures are for year end. Deposits include securities and negotiable certificates of deposit.
3. Postal savings interest rate on ordinary savings; after 1941, rate on the longest-term savings certificates.
4. Up to 1918, the bank interest rate on the Tokyo six-month time deposit (annual average); between 1919 and 1947, the rate on the *ko*-type fixed amount deposit determined by *Tokyo yokin rishi kyotei kiyaku* (Tokyo Deposit Interest Agreement Regulations) and converted into deposit interest after tax; after 1948, the rate on the longest-term time deposit determined by *Rinji kinri choseiho* (Temporary Law on Interest Rate Coordination).
5. Ratio to the preceding year.

Setting aside the Meiji period, when the financial system was by no means fully established, the ratio of postal savings to bank deposits stabilized in the vicinity of 15 percent in the second decade of the 20th century. Yet private financial institutions were rocked by the Great Depression and by the Japanese recession in the early Showa period, and postal savings started to account for a much larger share of deposits as banks began to fold or were merged. By 1944, postal savings accounted for 49.8 percent of bank deposits. Table 15 depicts the sharp drop in the numbers of banks during this period, from 1,541 in 1925 to only 65 in 1945. Table 3 in the preceding section also shows that it was not only postal savings that accounted for a growing share of deposits, but also small financial institutions like the agricultural cooperatives.

TABLE 15

HISTORICAL CHANGES IN THE NUMBER OF BANKS IN JAPAN

Year end	Commercial banks	Savings banks	Total
1926	1,417	124	1,541
1930	779	90	869
1935	466	79	545
1940	286	71	389
1941	186	69	255
1945	61	4	65
1950	67	--	67
1960	77	--	77
1970	76	--	76
1980	76	--	76
1987	77	--	77

Source: Bank of Japan, *Keizai tokei nenpo* (Annual report on economic statistics).

These rapid changes in the financial system during the Showa period reflected the global trend that followed the Great Depression of abandoning strict laissez-faire in favor of a mixed economic system. Yet they also were clearly part of the process by which the regime we know as the Japanese mixed economic system gradually took shape.

Although the hyper-inflation experienced in the latter half of the 1940s saw the ratio of postal savings to bank deposits drop to around 15 percent, it started to swell again during the high growth period of the late 1960s, reaching a ratio of 45.4 percent in 1985. In contrast to the pre-war period, post-war Japan has experienced no bank failures or mergers in the private sector. Consequently, there was seemingly no reason for postal savings to make large inroads into private-sector finance. Nevertheless, the rapid growth in the agriculture and regional economic sectors, as well as in middle-class income accompanying Japan's fast economic growth, probably worked to the advantage of the postal savings system. Its nation-wide, low-cost network (explained in detail below) and its popular savings instrument--the fixed-amount deposit--were well suited to take advantage of these trends. In any case, when taken in the context of the formation and maturation of the Japanese mixed economy, the significant expansion both before the war and during the high growth period in the share of postal savings and agricultural coops and so forth (albeit for different reasons) was a large and coordinated trend in the Japanese economy.

Major causes for the sharp jump in postal savings especially after the high growth period have been attributed in private financial circles to the cost advantage they allegedly enjoyed thanks to their nature as a government monopoly, or to the more favorable tax treatment they received compared with the private sector. Yet many of these analyses are based on mistaken premises.

First, the Postal Savings Special Account recorded an accumulating deficit for the late 1970s until the early 1980s, with the figure reaching ¥500 billion at the end of fiscal 1984. In this connection, it has been argued that the postal savings system has tried to expand its deposit-taking share through greater competitiveness by shifting the brunt of its hidden deficit over to postal operations and so forth. Yet this argument seems to be based on an insufficient acquaintance with the structure of the postal savings balance sheet.

Postal savings received primarily as fixed-amount deposits (six months maturity or longer) are basically redeposited with the Ministry of Finance's Trust Fund, mostly as long-term deposits of seven years or more. Accordingly, fund raising operations take place on a short-term basis while the fund is managed on a long-term basis. The balance fluctuates according to the yield curve formed by interest rate outlooks at the time. Basically, the balance sheet goes into the black in low-interest periods and into the red in high-interest periods. The balance sheet is further unsettled at times of interest rate volatility due to the time lag between the receipt and conferral of funds. In fact, the balance has improved since low interest rates became the pattern in 1985, and the accumulated deficit has been eradicated. Of course, the postal savings system is able to shoulder such long-term interest rate fluctuation risk precisely because it is in the government sector, but in the medium to long run its structure is one where a surplus is accumulated only to the extent that there is a long-term interest rate risk premium.

Further, as postal savings accounting is done as a general rule on a cash basis, a maximum of six months prepaid interest is not recorded. Accordingly, it has been pointed out that the postal savings deficit is larger than would appear and that expansion based on such a large deficit structure would be problematic at best. This apparent discrepancy, however, amounts to a divergence in the outstanding balance derived from different accounting principles. Although the shift over to an accrual basis would indeed cause an almost ¥1 trillion deficit, this would represent only a one-time event, not the start of a structural deficit. Moreover, although both postal savings and postal services derive some cost advantages from the proportional division of common facilities, there is no evidence that postal savings derive special benefit from this arrangement compared with other financial institutions.

Concerning the efficiency of postal savings operations, although the location of a large number of branches in residential areas where customers live would seem at first glance to represent an extremely inefficient investment, the rate of operating costs is extremely low--0.7 percent. Moreover, this figure has been falling swiftly in line with the increase in the absolute volume of postal savings in recent years. The main reason for this low rate of operating expenditure is the use of public servants--at a substantially lower cost than that of the staff of a typical large private financial institution--for labor-intensive work. Regarding capital investment, it is not unusual in the case of special post offices for the postmaster's own residence to be offered at low rental. This practice, plus the low pay scale of public employees and the prestige associated with this position in local communities, enables the system to save vast sums on compensation for senior managers.

It is these 18,000 special post offices that act as the backbone of postal savings operations in Japan, and the majority of postmasters see postal savings and not postal or postal insurance services as their main area of activity. In contrast, postal services are mainly carried out by special collection and delivery offices in conjunction with ordinary post offices, and postal insurance operations by agents at ordinary post offices. These three operational areas are therefore managed quite distinctly.

Postmasters for special post offices are often chosen on a hereditary basis, and are more often than not influential figures in their community. For this reason, the transfer of postmasters at special post offices is rare. Such stability allows for close relations with the local community, which in turn makes for a formidable ability to collect deposits at a grass-roots level. As influential members of the community, postmasters also wield considerable political power due to their ability to deliver votes at election time. A nation-wide organization that has substantial influence with the Liberal Democratic Party (LDP) also exists for postmasters at special post offices.

As is often pointed out, the jewel in the postal savings crown has so far been the fixed-amount deposit, an extremely competitive instrument in terms of both liquidity and yield in an environment of regulated deposit rates. Deposits made in periods of high interest rates continue to receive the same rate of interest for ten years. This feature enables postal deposits to serve a function similar to long-term government bonds. At the same time, the deposits can be withdrawn any time after six months at no capital loss. Needless to say, they are an extremely attractive investment instrument--especially in periods of high interest rates.

The fixed-amount deposit also enjoys considerable advantages over other long-term fixed-interest instruments in times of interest rate volatility or other economic uncertainties because it can be deposited on a short-term basis. Leaving aside the large depositor who has a choice of many instruments, continuing regulation of interest rates and limited choice for small deposits has made the fixed-amount deposit an extremely attractive instrument for the ordinary small depositor.

High interest rates can be locked in for ten years, or investors can opt for a floating rate--all according to their needs. Of course, the more advantageous for the depositor, the greater the burden on the postal savings side, but at least the fixed-amount deposit's superiority as a commodity has not resulted in a structural deficit for the post office to date.

It is also true in a certain sense that postal savings act as a tax shelter, but probably to no significantly greater extent than investment instruments at private financial institutions. Although the postal savings system is generally more lax than private institutions in checking the identity of account holders at the same branch, it takes a considerably harsher view of the opening of accounts under the same name at different branches. The tax authorities' view, however, seems to be "six of one, half a dozen of the other." Yet private financial institutions are subject to tax investigations and the post office is exempt, a fact that works to the advantage of postal savings in psychological terms.

In sum, the main causes for the sharp increase in postal savings both before and after the war lie in the system's government-backed, low-cost, nation-wide network, and in its ability under a regime of regulated interest rates to offer an overwhelmingly competitive instrument, the fixed-amount deposit. This capability has only been possible because of the official nature of the postal savings system, which functions as a strong competitor to private financial institutions.

The real issue here is whether it is desirable in terms of national economic efficiency that the public sector, with the inherent advantages it enjoys due to its official status, competes with the private sector. In the case of Japanese finance, the answer is yes. In the first place, the private sector enjoys several advantages over the public sector--for example, an ability to offer loans and issue bonds. Nor is the private sector at an overwhelmingly competitive disadvantage vis-a-vis the public sector, and it is extremely desirable from an efficiency point of view that competition exists between organizations with different objectives and functions.

Indeed, the public sector can play an important role as a countervailing power to the somewhat oligopolistic private financial institutions, especially when the financial system is highly regulated and has the kind of oligopolistic tendencies as Japan had throughout the Showa period. Had it not been for the current services provided to the small depositor by the postal savings system and the agricultural coops, the Japanese financial system would have become more biased towards big financial institutions and wholesale banking. Although there has not been much interest rate competition at the retail end, it is well known that non-price competition has been very tough, and it is undeniable that the existence of the postal savings system and the agricultural coops lies behind this competition. Compartmentalized competition between the public and private sectors is one of the major characteristics of the Japanese mixed economy, as demonstrated by the role of postal savings and agricultural cooperatives in the financial arena.

Anti-monopoly laws have been the American response to a market tendency towards monopoly or oligopoly centering on major corporations and the resultant disadvantages for the national economy. In Japan's case, however, direct engagement in the same activities by the public sector has played a useful role as a countervailing power. In the financial markets, postal savings, postal insurance, and agricultural coops have acted as the main countervailing powers in the deposit-taking sector. But as was shown in the preceding analysis, city, town, and village authorities, and often organically interconnected cooperatives, have also been a force of resistance to the monopolistic tendency of an economy dominated by large corporations. The role of the special post office postmaster within the postal savings system is more in the nature of a local cooperative chief. These officials are therefore deeply connected to the community and wield considerable political influence.

Although the postal savings system is closely linked to the local community, it is still directly operated by the state. On a more general level, however, a pattern in which local government acts as the hub of public sector works, or cooperatives act as works coordinators, is unfamiliar in the United States and Europe. In Japan, it is not unusual for representatives in local assemblies to be members of a major cooperative or to be public contractors. The administrative and executive branches of municipal bodies typically work as one coherent entity in carrying out public sector works.

Nor is there any shortage of cases where municipalities themselves are involved in business activities. Examples include Takachi City's Takachi Wine and Furano City's Furano Wine, both in Hokkaido, or the Oguni cedar development authority in Kumamoto Prefecture's Oguni Town. This, however, is more a new twist to the traditional role hitherto played by municipalities in the Japanese mixed economy than a wholly new trend towards regional decentralization.

This point is confirmed by some of the activities in which Oguni Town is currently engaged. The core of the "rehabilitation" project for Oguni cedar is "Yuki no Sato" Incorporated, which is being financed on a 50-50 basis as well as jointly managed by Oguni Town and the forestry cooperative. Carpenters under exclusive contract will be responsible for a comprehensive system covering everything from lumber production to housing construction, and they are currently building in Fukuoka their first traditional Japanese farmhouse for export.

Using its position as a public works instigator, the town is also constructing marketing and forwarding facilities for local products, as well as a local produce hall. The former is a market for livestock managed by the local agricultural cooperative. The construction contractor is the Agricultural Land Development Corporation. The livestock market is being constructed as a subcontract to a larger development project for regional agriculture. The local produce hall is a public facility owned by Oguni Town and is managed and operated by the same agricultural cooperative. Experimental manufacturing and marketing of butter, cheese, ham, and sausages under the agricultural cooperative brand name is being carried out. These facilities are being constructed with the help of central government and prefectural subsidies as part of a model scheme aimed at stemming the flow of young residents to the cities. The town is also actively proposing new ideas, such as constructing a municipal gymnasium and traffic center by applying reinforced steel rod construction methods to wooden structures.

The entrepreneur for this series of undertakings is the town mayor, Yoshitoshi Miyazaki. It was he who ordered the wooden gymnasium after coming across one made by a local architect in a magazine. The governor of Kumamoto Prefecture, Morihiro Hosokawa, also is very enthusiastic about these kinds of projects, and is said to have his sights set on creating a rural cultural zone. Although the prefecture subsidizes "biggest-best-first in Japan" projects like the above to the tune of ¥20 million per project per year, the great part of central government subsidies come with strings attached, which makes it difficult for new projects to benefit. Ever increasing central government red tape is also said to be a constant headache. Of course, Oguni Town has been lucky to have both a progressive mayor and governor in office. This has enabled the town to go ahead with more ambitious projects, but it is still the existing system that provides the overall framework, enabling politicians to take the initiative and to work in conjunction with the cooperative.

Another well known example is Kobe City, which has long been involved in such projects on an even grander scale. The number of actors involved in this system of public works, however, is extremely large. Enormous energy and political influence are required first to create a local consensus with the cooperatives and so on, and then to carry the project up the various ladders of prefectural and central government. In many cases, the services of the constituency's Diet representative are essential in cajoling the central bureaucracy into ensuring that subsidies and/or permits will be forthcoming.

Apart from the aforementioned national land improvement and postal savings operations, where involvement is direct, the central government's role in the public sector consists mostly of overseeing and managing--through the pertinent ministries, agencies, and their regional offices--public works undertaken on a city, town, and village level in conjunction with the prefecture. The central government also oversees and manages works undertaken on a prefectural level, and makes the necessary budgetary appropriations. In other words, although the actual implementation of projects by the public sector takes place on a very broad-ranging, decentralized basis, the supervisory powers of prefecture and central government have been kept fairly strong--mainly by budgetary control, the allocation of subsidies, and the authority to place projects on regional publics works accounts.

In some respects, this scheme resembles the internal organization of large Japanese corporations, where information and the authority to act is decentralized but personnel and financial power remains concentrated in the head office. Both types of organizations are fundamentally decentralized, bottom-up enterprises characterized by tight management and supervision. In the case of large private firms, however, the supervisory body is one-dimensional and this concentration of authority makes top-down activity possible at times. Supervision in the public sector, by contrast, is multi-dimensional and also affected by politics, which makes the top-down approach extremely difficult. Indeed, there is a much stronger possibility that checks on new projects will pop up to interfere at all possible levels, making it exceedingly difficult to change the status quo. It is precisely this state of affairs that Karel van Wolferen has criticized in his 1989 book, *The Enigma of Japanese Power*, arguing that the Japanese government is besieged by special interest groups; that its complex of overlapping hierarchies is capable of creating balance but not of making decisions; and that a Japanese Prime Minister has less power than the head of government of any Western country.[33]

In the previous section, small firms were described in terms of their subcontracting relationship to larger firms. Yet certain sections of the industries outside manufacturing--especially construction and service industries, like retailing at the local level--do not always have a business relationship with larger corporations. Such firms often organize themselves into some sort of grouping like a chamber of commerce and create a local economic domain far removed from the large corporations. These smaller firms often have stronger ties with the public sector than larger firms, and it is not unusual for them to be at the forefront of regional politics and administration. Political attempts to block expansion by larger companies, like the Large Retailers Regulatory Act, are mainly propelled by these smaller companies. Strong ties between the public sector and small, local retailers have made them one of the backbones of LDP support, alongside agriculture and the construction industry. The budget for small and medium companies administered by MITI's Small and Medium Enterprises Agency, as well as the LDP's commerce *zoku* representatives, act as the state pipeline for small and medium companies.[34]

In any event, although small Japanese firms are connected either to the large corporate sector or the public sector depending on their size and business sector, they remain relatively independent and form their own distinct group of businessmen in Japan. Yet the role of these entrepreneurs is only a minor one in the Japanese model of a mixed economy. The system's larger framework unmistakably is formed by the large corporate and public sectors. Still, the entrepreneurs of small firms inject a large dose of capitalistic energy into the system as a whole and provide it with its elasticity.

Politics as Business

"You can't get money out of the government when all you've got are representatives who think they're kingpins. You can't keep everyone happy unless you're prepared to lay your life on the line and go about overturning the desk of the Director General of the Budget Bureau at MOF!" At least, that is what Shin

---

[33]Van Wolferen, *op. cit.*

[34]Inoguchi and Iwai have developed an interesting analysis and named these commercial *zoku* representatives "hunting dog *zoku.*" See Takashi Inoguchi and Tomoaki Iwai, *Zoku Giin' no Kenkyu* (Nihon Keizai Shimbunsha, 1987).

Kanemaru[35] had to say in April, 1988 in a speech in Kikuchi City, Kumamoto Prefecture.

Kikuchi City is also where extensive agricultural works are being carried out under the Ministry of Agriculture and Fisheries' Special Account for National Land Improvement. At a total works cost of ¥20.9 billion and covering 4,740 hectares, this project was started in 1979 and is scheduled for completion in 1992, if fund appropriation goes smoothly. This area is renowned as a public works Mecca; the prefecture also is carrying out related works that cover 4,720 hectares, works by cooperatives covering 830 hectares, and the construction of Ryumon Dam (a project of the Ministry of Construction). Kanemaru's statement is worth noting as an unambiguous description of the politician's role in this region.

In the preceding section, it was argued that engineering works and financial activities form the core of public sector operations. With the exception of the postal savings system and other entities, however, more often than not it is prefectural and other local authorities or cooperatives that instigate these programs. Moreover, the role of the prefecture and the state in this system-- particularly the state--is to control these works indirectly by budgetary and financial means, and to oversee and supervise the city, town, village, or cooperative. Yet this supervision does not constitute a one-way, top-down system. Rather, it is based on mutual understanding between the region or cooperative directly in control of the project and the state. And significant influence in formulating this understanding is exerted by politicians involved on the national level. Kanemaru's statement is a clear indication that a Diet-man has to be prepared to resort to measures as extreme as overturning desks to build this consensus, if the need arises.

In this type of public system, then, annual budget compilation occupies a central place in policy formation. In areas directly administered by the government, such as foreign policy and defense, planning is the first problem; the budget only becomes important in relation to implementing policy. For civil engineering and other public works programs, however, the job of the central government is to allocate budget appropriations. Passive adjustment therefore dictates policy decisions.

---

[35]A key senior member of the LDP who has served as both Secretary General and Vice Chairman of the party. In September, 1992, Kanemaru was convicted of violating political fundraising regulations and lost his role as the party's most powerful faction leader.

The "real" job of the legislative branch of government is to draw up legislation, but let us now look at the actual role played by both politicians and government servants by clarifying the relationship between legislative behavior and the budget. Table 16 lists the number of bills enacted by the Diet in the post-war era.

TABLE 16

NUMBERS OF BILLS ENACTED AFTER THE WORLD WAR II

Year	Numbers	Year	Numbers	Year	Numbers
1947	236	1963	182	1979	72
1948	287	1964	185	1980	115
1949	277	1965	145	1981	95
1950	290	1966	164	1982	103
1951	314	1967	147	1983	81
1952	313	1968	111	1984	78
1953	334	1969	97	1985	119
1954	228	1970	146	1986	110
1955	196	1971	147	1987	115
1956	179	1972	131		
1957	185	1973	118		
1958	189	1974	124		
1959	223	1975	98		
1960	172	1976	85		
1961	238	1977	91		
1962	164	1978	113		

After reaching a peak of 334 bills in 1953, the year following Japan's independence, the number of bills enacted has declined more or less steadily to 115 in 1987. Many of the so-called basic laws that form the basis of the post-war policy regime were enacted by 1953--e.g., the Constitution (1946), the Finance Act (1947), the Public Accounting Act (1947), the Diet Act (1947), the Cabinet Act (1947), the Local Government Act (1947), the Construction Standards Act (1948), and the Agricultural Land Act (1952). Since the process of fundamental government restructuring was completed by 1953, both the number of bills submitted and enacted subsequently began to fall. This downward trend was interrupted twice, however, between the late 1950s and early 1960s, and during the first half of the 1970s--that is, at the start and at the end of Japan's high economic growth period. The number of bills then resumed its decline as Japan's socioeconomic system became increasingly stable.

Table 17 gives some details of the bill enactment records of recent Diet sessions.

TABLE 17

DIET ENACTMENTS BY TYPE OF SESSION AND BUDGET RELATION, 1975-87

		Major Session		
Year	Total Enactment	Total	Cabinet-proposed	Budget-related
1975	98	67	48	25
1976	85	69	59	31
1977	91	76	65	34
1978	113	95	83	34
1979	72	53	45	30
1980	115	85	75	33
1981	95	89	72	39
1982	103	98	79	35
1983	81	60	52	29
1984	78	78	70	40
1985	119	100	85	36
1986	110	85	73	33
1987	115	81	72	41

The Table subdivides enactments between major (or budget) sessions and others, as well as between budget-related and unrelated bills. The major or budget session is normally convened in late December and lasts 150 days--sometimes longer in the case of extended sittings. Depending upon the year, there may be one or two temporary sessions, during which a supplementary budget is delivered. Under normal conditions, however, Diet proceedings pivot around debates on budget appropriations. As can be seen from Table 17, 80 percent of bills enacted are submitted at major sessions, 90 percent of which are submitted by the Cabinet and 50 percent of which are budget-related bills. A bill's relation to the budget is determined by the rather strict criterion of whether it directly affects budget figures or not. In many cases, even bills officially classified as not budget-related have some indirect bearing on the budget. Apart from international treaties and virtually automatically renewed bills that must be enacted by a certain date, the so-called debates on budget-related bills have priority over debates on unrelated bills.

In other words, a substantial portion of the bills enacted in the Japanese Diet are related in some way to the budget, and the passage of budget appropriation bills and budget-related bills is given the utmost priority. In fact, the Budget Committee is considered the most important Diet committee, and all Cabinet members are expected to be present regardless of the specific topic of the day's debate--meaning that the meetings are not held that often. This means that other committees cannot be convened when the Budget Committee is in session because Cabinet ministers cannot attend. It is also customary for each committee to convene only twice a week, and although the number of days in a Diet session is just as long as, or even longer than, those in its European and U.S. counterparts, the number of hours spent actually discussing each bill is relatively short.

Several empirical studies of course have already pointed out the fallacy of the view that the brevity of actual discussion means that Diet debate simply endorses LDP government policy. The refusal of any party to debate can lead to a suspension of discussions because Japanese convention dictates that the Diet be run by a consensus, not by majority rule. Bulldozing legislation through is deemed an infraction of the rules, even by the media, and the opposition parties exercise considerable power in this respect.

Because of these conventions, timetables take on a paramount importance in the Diet. Will there in fact be enough time, no matter how short, to actually discuss proposed bills? It is precisely from these time constraints that the Diet House Management Committee and the Diet committees from each party derive a decisive role in the Diet deliberative processes. For both the government and the ruling party, it is crucial that the budget and its related bills be passed during the 150-day-long major session. As it had the necessary majority to pass bills each year from 1953 until 1989, more often than not the discussions that took place in the Diet were a mere formality, confirming the agreement reached between LDP and the government before the Diet session. The real challenge is sticking to the timetable. Answers to opposition questions are therefore defensive and veiled, and one of the government's major strategies is to avoid confrontation on key policy issues, as well as preventing suspension or procrastination by the opposition parties. It is this characteristic of Diet question-and-answer time that is probably the main reason for the "clearly spoken but ambiguous in meaning" replies made by the government.

Behind this budget oriented "viscosity" of the Diet[36] lies an extremely interdependent government bureaucracy and the dominant Liberal Democratic Party. In a certain sense, Diet discussions amount merely to last minute fine-tuning, or to a somewhat ritualistic confirmation of what has already been prepared by the government party apparatus during the six-month-long "budget season" preceding the major Diet session. The ritualistic nature of the discussions, however, does not make the process any less important. In fact, the process itself is so crucial that a misstep at any point can lead to the demise of a bill. This all-or-

---

[36]Mike Mochizuki, *Managing and Influencing the Japanese Legislative Process: The Roles of Parties and the National Diet* (Harvard University Press, 1982).

nothing situation differs sharply from that in the U.S. Congress, for example, where bills are debated at length and numerous amendments made.

The annual budget appropriation bill clearly dominates Japanese parliamentary processes. But how is the budget bill itself compiled? The budget process officially starts in late June, when discussions begin on aggregate figures or "ceilings" for requests in the major spending categories, such as general expenses and public works. Each spending ministry and the Ministry of Finance carry out a regular personnel reshuffle from mid- to late June, after the Diet closes, to prepare for the start of the budget season. Often a Cabinet reshuffle will also take place around this time. The paramount importance of timetables in parliamentary processes has already been mentioned, but the "calendar" for budget compilation is also crucial. With the schedule for the presentation of government proposals to the major session acting as the deadline, consultation and negotiation between the MOF, the spending ministries, and the LDP follow complex and intricate procedures, the sheer number of players involved ensuring that observing both correct sequence and ritual is extremely important. As a result, the timing of transfers of information is of decisive importance.

The first critical decision, at least in terms of macroeconomic policy, is the establishment of ceilings, and it is made within a relatively short period. In early July, the MOF prepares a ceiling draft for budget requests, negotiating and receiving agreement from the spending ministries and the LDP Executive Council by late July. The inevitable sanctioning of requests up to the ceiling constitutes the de facto determination of aggregate budget figures. Yet the brief, generally problem-free nature of this initial process only illustrates how much more important micro-level distribution is in Japanese politics and administration than the determination of overall volume on a macro plane.

Once they are advised on the ceiling for each spending category, the spending ministries then set about preparing their "policies" and detailed budget requests. Budget compilation is identified here with government policy, although the two obviously are different concepts. There are good reasons, however, to assume the dominance of budget compilation in government policy-making, hence the quotation marks. Each spending ministry scoops up requests from its respective regional offices and related government institutions, and also consults with the *zoku* representatives on the LDP's policy subcommittees (*Bukai*), as well as with other concerned organizations. The central government's role is not insignificant in the sense of thinking up new policy ideas or putting together an overall "policy" package. But as previously mentioned, many projects are instigated at the city, town, village, or local cooperative level. In these cases, the central bureaucracy does not make requests but rather fields them. Its job in a broad sense therefore resembles that of a coordinator.

The role of the members of the *Bukai* (*zoku* representatives) here is to lobby the central government on behalf of their local government and organizations, as well as to ensure that their demands are successfully incorporated into ministerial "policy." At another level of the budget compilation process, they also work very closely with each spending ministry and function as their lobbyists against the MOF. The MOF or government draft budget must ultimately be approved by the LDP's Executive Council and Policy Affairs Research Committee. Since the *zoku* lobbyists have close ties through party factions with the Council and Committee, or are themselves key officials, they occupy an extremely important position. Yet the relationships among the LDP, the MOF, and the spending ministries are by no means those of control and submission, but rather of complex interdependence. Chart 5 is an illustration thereof, albeit a somewhat oversimplified one.

CHART 5

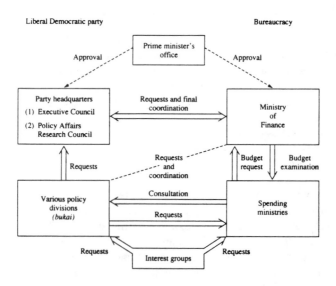

In a representational cabinet system, the Prime Minister is also the party president, and although the Prime Minister's will is important, in the long run even he is constrained by factional considerations and cannot go against strongly expressed will. Nor would it be wise for the bureaucracy to tackle the party head on. Yet to the extent that the spending ministries and the MOF act as the secretariat for "policy" and budget compilation, and thereby dominate the logistics thereof, the Prime Minister cannot afford to flaunt the will of the secretariat, either.

At the same time, the party-versus-bureaucracy schema often put forward by the mass media or academic circles is somewhat misleading. In view of the spending ministries' collaboration with the LDP *Bukai*, it would often be more useful to analyze the situation in terms of a pattern in which the MOF and the party bosses are pitted against the spending ministries and party *Bukai*. Bureaucratization of the LDP has proceeded rapidly since the 1960s, with power once concentrated in the party bosses becoming more widely distributed throughout the overall party structure. This process has strengthened the position of the so-called *zoku* representatives and has coincided with the greater politicization of the spending ministries, as well as with a relative decline in the MOF's powers. As a result, the budget compilation process has become much more decentralized and pluralistic.

Budget requests are finalized around late August or early September, and are formally submitted to and examined by the MOF from September to December. Of course, all the while, the major actors are busy carrying on various behind-the-scenes negotiations. The key channels, at least on the surface, run between the MOF and the spending ministries, with detailed policies and numbers being negotiated among them at the assistant director or director level. The process is extremely decentralized and highly cumulative. Assistant directors or directors in the spending ministries draw up "policy" proposals that come under their own jurisdiction, coordinate with the institutions concerned, and submit the resulting budget requests to the MOF. All necessary documentation and explanation of the "policies" must go through this channel. Although the accounting division of each spending ministry coordinates and oversees all the detailed requests from its own ministry, all requests originate either from the original section, or from the local government or cooperatives for which that section is responsible. As such, "policies" or budget requests are not created from the top-down. Moreover, the examination of and negotiation for budget requests basically takes place at assistant director (or director) level, any necessary briefing being made to more senior personnel. In the meantime, it is the job of the senior bureaucrats to consult with the *zoku* members of the *Bukai*, party bosses, and related institutions to generate a consensus.

It should be noted here that the role in this process of top government and party officials is basically passive. Actual negotiations over "policy" and budget are extremely decentralized and take place at assistant director (or director) level. Of course, assistant directors or directors will sound out their superiors on strategic points or may formulate proposals on the initiative of more senior bureaucrats, such as director-generals or vice-ministers. The initiative may even come not from the bureaucracy but from the party side. In any case, documentation is almost invariably carried out by the assistant director (or director) and the basic "policy"-making process, with some exceptions, is extremely decentralized and cumulative. This sort of decision-making process can also be found in large Japanese firms, but the public sector's methods of budget compilation are probably the most radical examples of their kind. Compared to this extreme, private sector firms would seem to have a greater concentration of authority and more top-down decision making.

Although public sector "policy" is coordinated on a departmental or ministerial level, it tends to be extremely meticulous because of the relatively narrow jurisdiction of the assistant director or director, and because of the section's role of coordinator rather than instigator. "Policy" is often too segmented and lacking in a grand vision or coherence. Moreover, since the path from local body to final adjustment is long and policy proposals are scrutinized by so many people, proposals themselves tend to become somewhat conservative and aim at preserving or patchworking the status quo. After all, any departure from the status quo would inevitably threaten someone's vested interests, thereby making it even more difficult to generate consensus among so many players. Lobbyists often manage to get special interests (or at least existing vested interests) woven into budget figures in some form or another, and their veto powers can be overruled only by a truly extraordinary force or event--e.g., foreign pressures. The basic premise of this drawn-out and intricate decision-making process is the paramount importance of consensus. Given the number of actors with the power of veto, it is not easy even for the Prime Minister to set his own initiatives in motion. According to van Wolferen, this is the crux of the "Japan problem."

Former Prime Minister Yasuhiro Nakasone, who aimed at a "presidential style" of politics, is said to have bypassed much of this decision-making mechanism and to have tried to implement top-down politics and administration. Nevertheless, the system remains largely unchanged by Nakasone's tenure. On the contrary, it is probably because his skillful management of the government and executive branches did not fundamentally change existing mechanisms that he was able to carry out several radical policies (e.g., privatization of the national railway and NTT). Nakasone's unusually long stay of five years in the Prime Minister's office and his all-out efforts for reform also probably contributed to his highly unorthodox policy decisions.

In any case, this cumulative budget-oriented policy-making process has only a one-year horizon. Consequently, initiating policies that take a longer view, or change the status quo, is quite difficult, if not impossible. In particular, structural reform has become increasingly difficult as both the LDP and its base of support have grown more institutionalized in the post-war era, and as interdependence between the LDP and the government bureaucracy has become more systematic. The establishment of firm career paths and the development of *zoku* representatives within the LDP as well as the institutionalization of local support groups have all contributed to the bureaucratization and institutionalization of the party.

A particularly important point is that interdependence between the *zoku* representatives and government bureaucracy is extremely strong and has become increasingly institutionalized. In the early stages of their political careers, representatives opt for specialization in one ministry or another, becoming members of the Diet committee and LDP policy research subcommittee related to that ministry and building up their base as "*zoku*." During the pursuit of their careers, these representatives cultivate their relationship with the ministry, thereby creating a stable, long-term interdependence. As mentioned earlier, a great many representatives act as the Tokyo treasury officer or lobbyist for municipal bodies or for public works in their districts, and in order to play this role, cultivating a strong relationship with the ministry is of the utmost importance.

At the same time, bureaucrats in the ministries actively welcome this kind of development because these politicians constitute a strong support unit and lobby for their "policies." Fielding local requests, they also act as a buffer between special interest groups and the ministry, and also wield considerable political clout vis-a-vis the MOF. Moreover, since LDP convention assures that these politicians will rise to the position of parliamentary vice minister or minister at some future date if re-elected enough, it is to the ministry's advantage to court those prospective ministry heads. Essential to note is that although the seniority system is a common feature of Japanese organization, it is within the LDP and not the corporate or bureaucratic sectors where it is observed most rigidly. (Strictly speaking, in the party's case it is not the number of years but the number of a Diet-man's terms that determines seniority.) It is the LDP's adherence to extremely conservative and impartial rules regarding personnel, the bottom line of any organization, that makes the party organization even more stable and bureaucratic in flavor than is commonly appreciated.

The frequent contacts and interactions between *zoku* representatives and bureaucrats closely resembles those of business partners. *Zoku* representatives essentially chase after votes and political contributions while ministries seek bigger budgets and more influence. True, both politicians and bureaucrats pursue "policy" aimed at the "national" interest, but only in an indirect way. Each ministry puts together its budget requests or "policy" in consultation with the *zoku* representative, who has already fielded requests from the constituency. Yet it is not clear whether the rules of coordination are weighted at the time to suit national, ministerial, or *zoku* interests. Of course, such rules are checked in the process of examining budget requests by the MOF, the Diet Policy Affairs Research Committee, LDP party headquarters, and the Prime Minister's Office. Coordination powers have traditionally been strong at the MOF and party headquarters and are still considerable. Given the increase in the political clout of other ministries and the institutionalization of *zoku* representatives, however, the MOF's coordinating role has been substantially weakened. In fact, the MOF and the party have often joined forces, with the MOF's weakening grip frequently being bolstered by intervention from the Prime Minister's Office, particularly under Nakasone.

The rise in the influence of *zoku* representatives' influence conversely has acted to strengthen the role of LDP party bosses vis-a-vis the MOF. In other words, it is often politically efficacious to keep the *zoku* under a tight rein in order to oppose their pet "policies," and it is only the party bosses who can do this. In reality, the coordination of key "policies" is often carried out by the Prime Minister, the minister of finance, and senior LDP officials. To the extent that both the Prime Minister and minister of finance are key party members, final coordination can be said to take place in the LDP. The party's role, however, is passive and often results in a middle-of-the-road approach--or as the Japanese saying puts it, "add then divide by two."

Generally speaking, coordination by either the MOF, the Prime Minister's Office, or senior party officials has become increasingly ineffective since the high economic growth period of the 1960s. Opposition to "policies" affecting the status quo can succeed if the necessary numbers are mustered, some examples being the revolt by "Viet Cong" representatives over rice price cuts in 1985 and the tax reform revolt by young representatives in 1987. Although such revolts could be put down had they broken out in the corporate or bureaucratic sector by a personnel reshuffle, appointments within the LDP have become formalized without a commensurate centralization of authority. In this sense, the party's bonding as an organization can be said to be relatively weak. That is precisely why neither the Prime Minister nor party headquarters can make rebels toe the party line unilaterally.

This situation exactly "parallels" the relationship between the central bureaucracy and municipal bodies, or between the public and large corporate sectors. The grand rule here is not one-way control and submission, but coordination based on "mutual understanding." In this sense, the decentralization of authority in the public sector is proof of a broad base of activity and vitality. The point at issue here, however, is whether a leadership core can be established to orchestrate this broad base. In the Japanese private corporate sector, the distribution of information and decentralization of business operations aimed at injecting enthusiasm into employees (or "firing them up") is counterbalanced by centralized authority over treasury and personnel decisions. This makes top-down responses to environmental changes possible. In the public sector, however, centralization over personnel matters was never strong and has gradually grown weaker. Let us look now at Table 18, a breakdown of the public works budget, as one example of the various rigidities in the public sector that have resulted from an increasingly ineffective coordination.

The public works budget is parceled out among five ministries and three agencies: the Ministries of Agriculture and Fisheries, Construction, Transportation, International Trade and Industry, and Welfare, the Hokkaido Development Agency, the Okinawa Development Agency, and the National Land Agency. It is a mammoth task to try and change their respective allocation shares. And as Table 18 shows, they have remained virtually unchanged for ten years. These figures are all the more shocking considering the rapid pace of change in the private sector during the same period. Even the slightest tinkering with these shares requires harnessing enormous political energy. To change them significantly has been far beyond the ability of either senior LDP party officials or the Ministry of Finance.

TABLE 18

PERCENT GENERAL PUBLIC WORKS BUDGET BY CATEGORY, 1979-87

Category	1979	1987
Agricultural infrastructure[1]	14.11	14.13
Irrigation[1]	13.55	13.72
Road construction	30.77	28.92
Housing	11.25	12.44
Sewerage	10.71	10.91
Forestry	4.53	4.56
Fishery	2.87	2.95
Port infrastructure	4.20	4.17

1. Both have been especially stable: agricultural infrastructure accounted for 14.1 percent every year from 1979-87 and irrigation for 13.6 percent, except in 1987, when it rose fractionally to 13.7 percent.

To sum up briefly:

1. Politics at the central level in Japan revolves around the compilation of the annual budget, and budget logistics dominate the LDP, its interaction with the ministries, and the ministries' interaction with each other.

2. "Policy" formulation is both a decentralized and cumulative process, with the LDP and the MOF playing no more than a passive, coordinating role in most cases.

3. Even the sections of the spending ministries responsible for "policymaking" are usually not the instigators of said policy. Thus, the actual act of "policymaking" is often a coordinating one.

4. Interdependence between the LDP and the government bureaucracy is extremely strong and has been increasing even more in recent years. Relations between *zoku* representatives and their ministries are both long-term and stable, and therefore closely resemble relations between large Japanese firms and their business partners.

5. The role of politicians in this process is to tend to the funding needs of their local "enterprises" and to lobby the central government on their behalf. In this sense, Japanese politicians have a much stronger "entrepreneurial" side than their European or U.S. counterparts. This trait owes largely to the nature of the Japanese public sector, which is dominated by public works and financial operations.

IV. The Establishment of a Mixed Economy à la Japonaise

First Moves Towards Establishing a "Mixed Economy"

Japan at the this time [the late 1920s] was already an established capitalist society . . . It is safe to say that the old-fashioned capitalism of the 19th century, that which Marx and Engels knew, still survived in Japan and the rest of the world about this time. Taking the United States for example, we see a tribe of wealthy capitalists in control: Rockefeller, the oil king, steel magnate Carnegie, railroad kings Harriman and Vanderbilt, Ford of automobile fame, and Morgan, supreme in the world of finance. An almost identical situation was to be found in Japan: large *zaibatsu* such as Mitsui, Mitsubishi, Sumitomo, and Yasuda were followed by a second tier of lesser *zaibatsu* such as Furukawa, Okura, Asano, Fujita, and Shibusawa. On a smaller scale, we find many individuals of considerable wealth, the so-called individual capitalists, who were active in the entrepreneurial sense. It is only natural that such wealthy capitalists should be concentrated in Tokyo and the Osaka-Kobe region, but there was also a considerable number of wealthy capitalists in regional cities and towns who supported local industry.

Takahide Nakamura, *Showa Keizaishi*[37]

---

[37]Iwanami Seminar Books 17 (Iwanami Shoten, February, 1986).

Although the flow of history is compartmentalized differently according to one's analytical focus, the usual approach for Japan's modernization process-- which commences with the Emperor Meiji (1868)--is to divide it into pre-World War II and post-World War II regimes. This pre-World War II/post-World War II division may be appropriate in the cases of the political system and of the electoral, parliamentary, and local government bodies that underwent substantial changes with the amendment of the so-called basic laws starting with the Constitution. Yet an analysis of the flow of economic events since Meiji points to another demarcation, namely that between the Meiji and Taisho eras (1868-1926), when classical capitalism was established, and the Showa period (1926-1989) when the Japanese model of a mixed economy gradually evolved.

Of course, even in terms of the economic system, the post-war reforms undeniably had a substantial effect on the regime. These reforms, however, clearly were an extension of the pre-war and war-time flow, and as such, did not represent an actual systemic shift. On the contrary, the real significance of the post-war reforms is that the absolute authority of the occupation force was able to solve overnight many of the difficulties that even the extraordinary circumstances of war, or Japanese military rule, had not. As already mentioned, what is more important from the standpoint of an economic system is the break-up of the *zaibatsu* in 1945-47 and the land reform of 1945-46. Both reforms can be said to have created the foundations for the Japanese mixed economic system because they were responsible for changing the basis of classical capitalism by (a) the effective dissolution of a capitalist tier and (b) the distribution of the means of production, i.e. land.

The shift from classical capitalism to mixed economy was a global trend brought on by the Great Depression and World War II. All the industrial countries made this shift to some extent. What makes the Japanese case stand out is the fact that classical capitalism was transformed under conditions of military defeat and occupation. In addition, both the pre- and post-war periods shared a strong move towards regionalism, physiocracy, and protection of existing industry with the formation of an extremely distinctive regional community and a throng of small and medium-sized companies.

It has already been mentioned that public works came to play a significant role, especially after World War II. This development would seem to indicate that, anticipating the global tide of Keynesian economics, the fiscal policy of pre-war Finance Minister Korekiyo Takahashi was, in a sense, institutionalized as the politico-administrative system in Japan.

The so-called *zaibatsu* are said to have been established in the early Meiji period as politically connected businesses or mining operations. Mitsui, Mitsubishi,

Yasuda, Okura, and Fujita belong in the first category, Sumitomo and Furukawa in the second. Even among the first group, however, groups such as Mitsui Miike, Mitsubishi Takashima, and Fujita Kosaka grew by investing in mining the money they made from political activities. These *zaibatsu* had firmly established their foundations by the end of Meiji (around 1910) and gradually grew after World War I.

According to Hidemasa Morikawa of the Hosei University Business School, the *zaibatsu* were marked by several characteristics not shared by their foreign counterparts.[38] First, families were not independent in Japan but were completely bound by the common will of an entire clan. The eleven Mitsui families and the 13 Yasuda families are a classic example, with no single family being allowed to manage its assets independently. Second, business management centered on modern industry was highly diversified as well as comprehensive. The *zaibatsu* compared favorably with their overseas counterparts, whose operations tended to be conservative and aimed at preserving their wealth.

The last significant distinction was that managers were given great authority and status. In *zaibatsu* such as Mitsui and Sumitomo, both of which go back as far as the Edo period (1603-1867), the right of management had been entrusted to the manager since that period. Even in the newer *zaibatsu*, the power of the professional manager gradually grew stronger as the initial generation of capitalist-managers retired. The backgrounds of these professional managers were diverse--from the typical *amakudari* ("descent from heaven") executives such as Eiichi Shibusawa (Ministry of Finance) and Morimasa Takei (Agriculture and Commerce Ministry), and Hikojiro Nakamigawa--nephew of Keio University founder Yukichi Fukuzawa--who studied at Keio and centered the management of his Mitsui *zaibatsu* on Keio men. But the common feature of these professional managers' backgrounds was that they were all products of the institutions of higher education established since Meiji.

In other words, although capitalists existed then, the original model for the post-war "salaryman executive" in the form of these professional managers predated even the dissolution of the *zaibatsu*. The Showa period can well be interpreted as a time in which these professional managers gradually increased their power and finally dislodged the capitalists. Table 19 was compiled by economist Yoshimatsu Aonuma of Keio University, and categorizes the career paths of managers over time.

---

[38]Hidemasa Morikawa, *Nihon Zaibatzushi* (Kyoikusha, 1980); *Nihon Keizaishi* (Nihon Keizai Shimbunsha, 1981).

TABLE 19

CAREERS OF MANAGERS BY INDUSTRY

| | Total | Fishery | Mining | Manufacturing | | | | | | | |
				Total	Food	Cotton	Textiles Other	Petro-chem-icals	Metal and steel	Machi-nery	Other
1900											
Total	1,000	--	35	205	43	52	45	22	--	33	10
Owner type											
Entrepreneur	59	--	2	9	2	0	3	0	--	2	2
Self-employed	374	--	12	90	19	26	26	9	--	5	5
From commerce	333	--	12	82	14	26	26	9	--	5	2
Family managers	50	--	2	--	--	--	--	--	--	--	--
Subtotal	488	--	16	99	21	26	29	9	--	7	--
Employee type											
Permanent employee	43	--	2	--	--	--	--	--	--	--	--
Outside the firm	78	--	--	14	2	--	2	2	--	8	--
From other firms											
Banks	76	--	8	9	2	--	--	--	--	7	--
Other	94	--	5	31	9	14	2	4	--	2	--
Not identified	219	--	4	52	9	12	12	7	--	9	3

(Continued)

TABLE 19

CAREERS OF MANAGERS BY INDUSTRY

	Electricity and Gas	Transportation	Commerce		Banking		Insurance	Other
			Trading Firms	Others	Specialized	Others		
1900								
Total	19	120	43	48	16	359	75	50
Owner type								
Entrepreneur	--	2	5	2	--	35	2	--
Self-employed	7	48	9	15	2	146	33	10
From commerce	7	28	7	15	2	139	31	10
Family managers	--	--	13	2	--	31	--	2
Subtotal	7	50	27	19	2	212	35	12
Employee type								
Permanent employee	--	4	2	2	2	23	--	8
Outside the firm	--	14	--	5	7	22	14	--
From other firms								
Banks	2	10	--	5	--	28	5	7
Other	8	6	--	2	--	20	5	9
Not identified	2	36	14	15	5	51	16	14

(Continued)

TABLE 19

CAREERS OF MANAGERS BY INDUSTRY

| | Total | Fishery | Mining | Manufacturing | | | | | | | |
| | | | | Total | Food | Textiles | | Petro-chemicals | Metal and steel | Machinery | Other |
						Cotton	Other				
1928											
Total	1,000	8	22	451	112	128	94	36	24	60	--
Owner type											
Entrepreneur	32	--	--	20	14	4	--	2	--	--	--
Self-employed	86	2	--	52	8	18	10	2	4	10	--
From commerce	50	0	--	40	6	14	8	0	4	8	--
Family managers	56	--	2	22	8	2	8	--	--	4	--
Subtotal	174	2	2	94	30	24	18	4	4	14	--
Employee type											
Permanent employee	180	--	4	68	16	32	8	4	--	8	--
Outside the firm	110	--	4	42	12	2	6	12	2	8	--
From other firms											
Banks	98	--	--	40	8	16	8	--	--	8	--
Others	221	--	12	114	22	26	26	14	12	14	--
Not identified	214	4	--	96	24	28	28	2	6	8	--

(Continued)

TABLE 19

CAREERS OF MANAGERS BY INDUSTRY

	Electricity and Gas	Transportation	Commerce		Banking		Insurance	Other
			Trading Firms	Others	Specialized	Others		
1928								
Total	97	74	22	20	56	98	82	16
Owner type								
Entrepreneur	--	2	--	--	--	--	--	4
Self-employed	2	2	6	2	--	4	14	2
From commerce	2	2	6	2	--	2	8	2
Family managers	8	2	--	8	2	8	2	--
Subtotal	10	6	6	10	2	12	16	6
Employee type								
Permanent employee	10	12	4	--	21	32	14	--
Outside the firm	16	16	--	--	20	8	2	--
From other firms								
Banks	4	6	--	4	6	18	18	--
Others	18	12	8	6	--	8	18	4
Not identified	34	22	1	--	4	20	11	6

(Continued)

TABLE 19

CAREERS OF MANAGERS BY INDUSTRY

	Total	Fishery	Mining	Manufacturing							
				Total	Food	Textiles		Petro-chemicals	Metal and steel	Machinery	Other
						Cotton	Other				
1962											
Total	1,000	11	29	597	79	36	38	129	123	176	16
Owner type	115	3	3	78	18	4	3	13	12	25	3
Permanent employee	465	3	19	240	32	20	18	49	47	68	6
Outside the firm	54	1	--	37	4	1	1	8	7	15	1
Employee type											
From other firms											
Banks	93	1	1	58	4	1	3	11	14	21	1
Others	245	2	5	166	18	10	12	43	41	38	4
Not identified	29	1	1	18	3	--	1	5	2	6	1

(Continued)

TABLE 19

CAREERS OF MANAGERS BY INDUSTRY

	Electricity and Gas	Trans-port-ation	Commerce		Banking		Insur-ance	Other
			Trading Firms	Others	Special-ized	Others		
1962								
Total	31	52	27	13	11	57	46	57
Owner type	--	3	1	3	--	--	--	15
Permanent employee	8	27	17	6	8	43	38	19
Outside the firm	2	7	--	--	1	--	1	3
Employee type								
From other firms								
Banks	--	3	1	1	2	11	4	5
Others	20	10	7	3	--	2	3	12
Not identified	1	2	1	--	--	1	--	3

Source: Yoshimatsu Aonuma, "Japanese Managers' Class," *Nikkei Shinsho,* pp. 151-152.

Whereas owner-managers accounted for some 50 percent of all managers in 1900, by 1928 their share had dropped to just under 20 percent, and fell to just over 10 percent by 1962. In the post-war period, within the so-called hired managers group, life-time hired managers accounted for the great majority, totaling just under 50 percent of all managers. In short, between 1900 and 1962, the positions of owner-managers and life-time hired managers had reversed themselves.

In the early Showa period, then, the *zaibatsu* groups that formed huge concerns were beginning to take shape and show signs of more conservative business development. Yet both the world and Japanese economies were in the throes of depression, and a popular backlash against these increasingly conservative *zaibatsu* was mounting as the agricultural sector became more impoverished and the economy declined. The so-called reformist bureaucracy, the military, and the press fanned this backlash, and anti-*zaibatsu* feelings were steadily fed by their criticism of "treacherous" acts involving Mitsui Bank and Mitsui Bussan running up the dollar with their dollar buying operations in 1930-31 (a form of foreign exchange hedging against Britain's abolition of the gold standard). The March, 1932 assassination of Mitsui's chairman, Ikuma Dan, by ultra-rightists vividly illustrates the heightened public antagonism at the time.

In response, the *zaibatsu* implemented a large "about-face" and overhauled their operations. Mitsui, which had been singled out for the most vociferous--and violent--attacks, executed a whole series of countermoves, once Nariakira Ikeda became the head director in September, 1934. The influence of the Mitsui family was weakened by the retirement of various family members from Mitsui companies and the public sale of stocks from other companies, while the social nature of the *zaibatsu* and the authority of management experts was increased. In fact, the *zaibatsu* showed a propensity to go with the trend of rapprochement with the military and reformist bureaucrats, and with a greater government tilt toward heavy industry as well as toward more intervention in the economy as a whole. The American occupation authorities viewed the military and *zaibatsu* as one and the same and proceeded therefore to dissolve the *zaibatsu*. Yet the pre-war cooperation with the military by the old *zaibatsu* was not necessarily spontaneous, and no little part of their about-face can be attributed to public and terrorist pressure.

Of course, this about-face was not caused by such pressure alone. It took place in the context of rapid changes in the country's economic structure caused by a shift in government policy. Specifically, the government responded to the Great Depression, and to escalating public unrest arising from frequent disputes between landowners and tenant farmers, by sharply increasing regional and rural public assistance. This new policy took two basic forms: first, "Opportune Assistance

Programs" (*Jikyoku Kyokyu Jigyo*); and second, general countercyclical measures such as raising public spending as a whole and lowering interest rates. These programs collectively were known as the "Takahashi fiscal policy," after the then Minister of Finance. Economic historian Takahide Nakamura of Ochanomizu University explained the thrust of this new policy:

Takahashi intuitively preempted the most important conclusion of Keynes "General Theory" in 1929. The nature of the policy he implemented can be summed up as follows. First, he let the exchange rate fall for the time being. As a result, the Japanese exchange rate with the United States dropped from just over $49 to ¥100 in 1931 to just under $20 as of the end of 1932, settling down at just over $30 in the spring of 1933 (vis-a-vis the United Kingdom, the rate settled at one shilling two pence to ¥100). This corresponded to approximately a 40 percent devaluation and, needless to say, contributed to an increase in exports. Second, on the domestic front, interest rates were slashed. The Bank of Japan commercial bills discounting rate--the official discount rate--fell from its 1931 peak of 5.8 percent to 3.65 percent by 1933. Third was the expansion of public expenditure, with general account expenditure growing from ¥1.47 billion to ¥1.95 billion from 1931-32 and swelling even further in 1933 to total ¥2.26 billion. Increased expenditure centered mainly on higher military expenditure (from ¥460 million in 1931 to ¥690 million in 1932 and ¥870 million in 1933) and greater agriculture-related public works s (the Opportune Assistance Programs, which were funded at ¥180 million in 1932, ¥210 million in 1933, and ¥160 million in 1934). A system of Bank of Japan-underwritten issues for public bonds was introduced to cover the government's shortage of funding resources.[39]

This was viewed as a classic example of an expansion in inflationary military spending arising from public bond issues underwritten by the Bank of Japan. In the New Finance Act enacted in the post-war period (1947), in line with this interpretation, Bank of Japan underwriting was deemed illegal. In fact, this doctrine formed the basic underpinning of the Act. Yet under the depressed economic conditions that existed in the 1930s, and bearing in mind the failure of market mechanisms, Takahashi's fiscal policy was revolutionary in promoting a mixed economic system well before the Keynesian school gained eminence. Certainly, it did encourage militarism and set Japan gradually on the path to World War II. But as has also been shown in--Table 20--the economy recovered smoothly without any serious inflation, and the average real growth rate for the years 1931-36 reached 6.2 percent. From 1934 on, when the economy was well on the way to recovery, Takahashi tried to prevent inflation by keeping army demands for increased expenditure to a bare minimum. This policy, however, elicited sharp

---

[39]Nakamura, *Showa Keizaishi-Sono Seicho to Kozo, op. cit.,* p. 125

TABLE 20

ECONOMIC INDICATORS OF THE 1930s

		Composition of GNP (Millions of Yen)						Surplus of the Nation on Current Account	Real GNP (1934-1936 price)	Price (1934-38=100)		Terms of Trade (1934-38=100)			
	GNE	Consumption	Government Current Balance	Government Fixed Investment	Private Fixed Investment	Export	Import			Consumer Price Index	Wholesale Price Index	Yen per U.S. Dollar	Net Terms of Trade	U.S. Import Price from Japan	U.S. Wholesale Price
1929	16,286	11,782	1,612	1,210	1,620	3,300	3,223	77	13,735	116.2	107.5	2.17	164	249.6	121.3
1930	14,671	10,850	1,452	1,010	1,329	2,486	2,439	47	13,882	104.4	88.5	2.03	151	198.5	110.0
1931	13,309	9,754	1,685	902	1,058	2,029	2,105	-76	13,941	92.4	74.8	2.05	154	152.3	92.9
1932	13,660	9,804	1,839	1,093	971	2,466	2,479	-13	14,557	93.4	83.0	3.56	130	89.3	82.5
1933	15,347	10,850	2,046	1,194	1,310	3,092	3,107	-15	16,025	96.3	95.1	3.97	119	94.8	84.0
1934	16,966	12,097	2,005	1,237	1,715	3,580	3,639	-59	17,422	97.6	97.0	3.39	103	99.9	95.4
1935	18,298	12,668	2,117	1,354	2,006	4,158	3,991	167	18,366	100.1	99.4	3.50	96	95.8	101.8
1936	19,324	13,328	2,183	1,427	2,209	4,580	4,389	191	18,763	102.4	103.6	3.45	101	104.3	102.9
1937	22,823	15,121	2,609	2,482	3,195	5,401	5,969	-568	19,949	110.4	125.8	3.47	98	119.6	109.9

Source: Nakamura (1978), pp.. 127-128.

criticism from the military, with Takahashi finally being assassinated by right-wing army officers during the coup of February 26, 1936.

Takahashi's subsequent fiscal policy became a textbook case of Keynesian macroeconomic stimulus, and it is astonishing to realize that these bold policies had already been implemented five years before the *General Theory* was published. It is clear, however, that regional promotion and rural assistance based on a program of public works was compatible with the shape of Japanese politics and administration since Meiji, and also with the ideas of the Seiyukai, one of the two major pre-World War II political parties. A more than sufficient base for the bold implementation of a "Keynesian" policy of public works programs existed at this time, when the tide of physiocracy was becoming extremely strong especially after the Showa Depression and the rural depression, and when regional poverty was becoming a major social issue.

Rather than representing a one-time measure to counter the recession, Takahashi's dramatic shift in policy shaped the Japanese public sector for years to come. It was pointed out in the preceding chapter that one of the more pronounced characteristics of the Japanese public sector was the extremely large proportion of public works carried out by regional government or by cooperatives. This pattern of regionally run public works was energetically pursued by the combined forces of Prime Minister Kei Hara and his Seiyukai party, and Finance Minister Takahashi, from the time of the first Hara Cabinet in 1918. Regional expenditure grew to reach its current share of the budget by about the mid-1930s.

Table 21 gives a breakdown of central and regional government fiscal expenditure for the years 1920-36, and shows that the central government share fell 15 percent during this period. Elsewhere, the ratio of spending by prefectures (including the Metropolitan Area) to spending by cities also soared, with total city expenditure increasing to one-fourth of total national spending. For reference purposes only, in fiscal 1986, the respective shares of total spending represented by central and regional government fiscal expenditure were only 38.2 percent and 61.8 percent, respectively--which points to further post-war progress in the regional dispersion of expenditure.

TABLE 21

COMPOSITION OF CENTRAL AND LOCAL GOVERNMENT EXPENDITURES

Year	Total of Central and Local Govts (¥ Mill.)	Central Govt (¥ Mill.)	Local Govt (¥ Mill.)	Prefectures (¥ Mill.)	Cities (¥ Mill.)	Towns and Villages (¥ Mill.)	Central Govt (%)	Prefectures (%)	Cities (%)	Towns and Villages (%)	Net Expenditures of General Accounts of Central and Local Govts (¥ Mill.)
1919	2,322.8	1,359.9	962.9	285.2	272.5	357.9	58.5	12.3	11.7	15.4	2,170.5
1920	2,582.6	1,489.8	1,092.8	323.8	324.5	386.9	57.7	12.5	12.6	15.0	2,408.7
1921	2,638.7	1,429.6	1,209.1	374.1	287.6	455.4	54.2	14.2	10.9	17.3	2,530.5
1922	2,634.1	1,521.0	1,113.1	407.2	420.5	264.0	57.7	15.4	16.0	10.2	2,528.8
1923	2,952.6	1,625.0	1,327.6	414.6	452.1	439.3	55.0	14.1	15.3	14.9	2,692.2
1924	2,954.3	1,524.9	1,429.4	409.7	547.6	451.9	51.6	13.9	18.5	15.3	2,694.0
1925	3,196.8	1,578.8	1,618.0	449.3	644.4	500.3	49.4	14.0	20.1	15.7	2,895.5
1926	3,766.5	1,765.7	2,000.8	492.2	936.3	540.8	46.9	13.1	24.9	14.3	3,420.1
1927	3,739.4	1,814.8	1,924.6	491.2	841.7	560.8	49.5	13.8	20.6	15.2	3,366.1
1928	3,474.0	1,736.3	1,737.7	489.5	695.5	529.6	49.2	13.3	21.5	15.2	3,155.1
1929	3,332.8	1,557.8	1,775.0	478.2	776.4	498.1	46.7	14.4	23.3	14.9	3,033.0
1930	3,123.1	1,476.8	1,646.3	502.6	634.4	488.9	47.3	16.1	20.3	15.6	2,841.0
1931	4,025.6	1,950.1	2,075.5	779.6	730.4	543.7	48.4	19.3	18.1	13.5	3,405.0
1932	5,082.3	2,254.6	2,827.7	987.0	1,270.4	547.1	44.3	19.4	25.0	10.7	4,315.0
1933	4,628.3	2,163.0	2,465.3	857.7	1,044.5	539.6	49.2	21.5	16.8	11.9	4,014.0
1934	4,606.1	2,206.4	2,399.7	857.3	959.7	560.3	50.0	19.8	17.2	12.4	4,752.0
1935	5,292.1	2,282.1	3,010.6	1,013.0	1,403.6	570.6	49.1	19.1	18.9	12.5	4,463.0

Sources: Takahide Nakamura, "Takahashi Zaisei to Kokyo Toshi Seisaku" Nakamura (1981), page 121.

As has been explained, however, transfers from the central government in the form of regional subsidies, regional tax allocations, national treasury disbursements, special traffic safety grants, and so on have been significant during the post-war period, reaching ¥20.6779 trillion, or 34.6 percent of total government expenditure in fiscal 1986. And the influence of these national transfers has conversely been growing stronger. Although this trend corresponds to a regional dispersal of public works and centralization of the budget, the central government share of national spending in fiscal 1986 was only 49.1 percent, or 10 percent lower than in 1920, even with transfers added into the expenditure breakdown. In other words, it would not be wrong to say that the Hara-Takahashi policy continues down to the present day, despite important systemic changes made in the post-war period. Adding in the transfers portion, it would seem that the policy of regionally dispersing expenditure received a further stimulus from post-war reform.

Moreover, Table 22 clearly shows that this rapid dispersal of expenditure to the regions was largely carried out by an increase in regional public and civil engineering works. In the period 1919-36, total costs for civil engineering and industry promotion (including rural engineering works) increased six-fold, to just under ¥6 trillion. As the 1985 accounts show, public works totalled ¥9.7634 trillion, or 21 percent of total regional government expenditure. This figure is almost identical to the 23 percent share of regional finance accounted for by civil engineering and industry promotion expenditure in 1935. Although there are several differences in the public finance system and in the nature of specific spending categories, it must be emphasized that the current shape of public-works-centered regional politics was more or less in place by 1935.

TABLE 22

CIVIL ENGINEERING AND NEW PROJECTS EXPENDITURES IN LOCAL FINANCE

	Total	Prefectures	Cities	Towns and Villages
1919	104	71	14	26
1920	213	116	35	35
1921	243	134	35	40
1922	304	156	43	54
1923	283	163	62	45
1924	289	167	59	49
1925	301	155	88	47
1926	347	171	111	52
1927	404	177	159	53
1928	432	186	174	68
1929	354	177	105	59
1930	320	167	94	49
1931	343	191	89	53
1932	569	354	90	124
1933	590	363	97	130
1934	533	332	95	107
1935	548	336	108	104
1936	589	338	84	87

Sources: Takahide Nakamura, *Takahasi Zaisei to Kokyo Toshi Seisaku* (1981), p. 122

Irrespective of his own personal intentions, after 1934, another feature of Takahashi's economic policy was the encouragement of heavy industrialization against a backdrop of burgeoning military expenses. The framework of government and private-sector interaction in the post-war Japanese economy was constructed in quick succession with (a) the establishment of a cooperative system between the "converted" *zaibatsu* and the government, (b) the development of new technology centered on military demand and the emergence of a whole new group of companies, (c) the establishment of a regulated financial system, and (d) the enactment of legislation covering many industrial sectors, such as the Oil Industry Act. Coupled after the war with the establishment of a corporate in-house system of employee sovereignty and professional managers that was brought about by the dissolution of the *zaibatsu*, these policies led to the gradual formation of the large corporate sector that played such a key role in Japan's post-war growth.

This war-time system, however, gave priority to military demand and was highly subject to bureaucratic control. As such, the relationship between the public sector and large corporations was much closer at this time than in the ensuing post-war period. Even under the abnormal conditions of war, the relative power wielded by corporate managers had not been emasculated to any significant extent. Nevertheless, these managers elected to follow a conciliatory path with the military and reform bureaucrats due mainly to the increase in anti-*zaibatsu* sentiment. The 1937 cabinet led by the militarist Senjuro Hayashi, was established to implement the Army's "Five Year Plan for Key Industries." It included Toyotaro Yuki from banking circles as the Finance Minister and Nariakira Ikeda as Governor of the Bank of Japan, and is an excellent example of this "conciliatory" stance. Ikeda, who along with Ikuma Dan was targeted by ultra-rightists, had embarked on reforming the Mitsui *zaibatsu* and probably chose to cooperate with the military in order to give Mitsui a chance of staying afloat.

Meanwhile, as Nakamura has shown, heavy industrialization in Japan was making rapid progress from 1930 on as well. As is evident from Table 23, the 1930s saw a sharp jump in the production of steel, automobiles, machine tools, and induction motors, but a levelling off of output in the light industries such as raw silk thread and cotton products. The production of ammonium sulfate, caustic soda and other chemical products, cement, sheet glass, and so on also skyrocketed. Meanwhile, heavy industrialization was further supported by revolutionary changes in technology. Backed up by growth in the power-generating industry, new technologies and new industries developed in quick succession, as shown by the sudden rise to power of the aluminum industry, the development of automobile manufacturers like Nissan and Toyota, and the emergence of airplane manufacturers like Nakajima Aviation and Mitsubishi Heavy Industry. The vitality of new technologies and industries was quite closely linked to military demand in Western countries as well during this period and thereafter, and in this sense, there was nothing unusual about the Japanese situation. Referring to this point, however, Nakamura does raise the following doubts as to whether military demand was absolutely essential or not.

TABLE 23

PRODUCTION OF MAJOR MANUFACTURED GOODS

Year	Cotton Textiles (Square Meters)	Raw Silk (1,000 Tons)	Metals (1,000 Tons)	Metal Vessels (1,000 Tons)	Autos (1,000)	Machine Tools (1,000)	Inductive Electric Machines (1,000)	Ammonium Sulfate (1,000 Tons)	Caustic Soda (1,000 Tons)	Cement (1,000 Tons)
1924	--	21.90	811	487.0	--	--	--	80.1	4.11	1,217
1929	2,140	31.10	1,300	48.2	--	--	--	131.1	25.4	2,292
1930	2,187	42.60	2,289	206.1	0.37	2.25	77.5	265.8	38.8	3,237
1935	3,438	43.70	4,704	141.9	5.33	10.10	148.9	611.8	245.1	5,683
1940	2,194	42.80	6,856	307.2	37.80	58.10	185.7	110.9	406.5	6,085
1945	46	5.22	1,963	607.6	6.90	7.32	116.4	243.0	56.8	929
1950	1,289	10.60	4,839	227.0	31.60	4.04	366.5	150.2	194.8	4,462
1955	2,523	17.40	9,408	502.4	68.90	18.10	666.8	212.9	501.8	13,024
1960	3,222	18.00	22,138	180.7	48.20	80.10	550.6	242.3	868.6	22,537

(Continued)

TABLE 23

PRODUCTION OF MAJOR MANUFACTURED GOODS

Year	Pulp (1,000 Tons)	Plate Glass (1,000 Boxes)	Synthetic Fiber (1,000 Tons)	(Reference) Domestic Gross Fixed-Capital Formation	
				Government Non-military (1934-36 Prices- ￥Mill.)	Private (1934-36 Prices- ￥Mill.)
1924	--	--	0.09	782(401)	1,799
1929	508	--	1.45	952(680)	1,326
1930	636	2,252	16.9	1,121(813)	1,102
1935	770	3,448	101.6	1,483(833)	2,257
1940	1,155	4,282	98.0	3,064(672)	7,462
1945	243	408	2.55		
1950	749	3,783	46.8		
1955	1,907	6,650	88.6		
1960	3,531	12,426	142.8		

Source: Nakamura (1978), pp. 129-130.

It has always been stated that military demand was the only engine of economic development at this time in the thirties, but we see these kinds of new industries emerging one after the other accompanied by plant and equipment investment. Steel for one, or oil for another, all in a certain sense can be called industries of military demand, but at the same time, there also existed the possibility of demand expanding in areas unrelated to the military machine, just as we see in Japan today. In actual fact, more than 80 percent of steel demand in the mid-thirties came from the ordinary private sector, with civil engineering and machinery accounting for more than half of demand. As can be seen from this example, it seems that various possibilities still remained. Although it seems highly unlikely, I believe that if the war had not taken place, the necessary components for a gentle transition to the post-war economy already existed within both the economy itself and industry as well.[40]

The development of a new industrial structure at this time pivoted around the so-called "newly risen concerns." Hidemasa Morikawa maintains that these corporate groups were not *zaibatsu* in the strictest sense.[41] Instead, they were groups where the shareholdings of related owners were low (even at Nissan, which had the strongest *zaibatsu* nature, the Ayukawa family's holdings accounted for only 5 percent in 1937), that were led mainly by technicians, and that by virtue of their technological enthusiasm were pioneering new fields. The majority of these concerns were linked to the military and reform bureaucrats, who displayed a healthy dislike for the established *zaibatsu*. They expanded substantially due to public demand and played a significant role as a countervailing power to the old *zaibatsu*. Nobuteru Mori of Showa Denko and Chikuhei Nakajima of Nakajima Aviation were also politicians and therefore in a position to maximize their contacts with both the military and the government.

The greatest weakness of these new concerns vis-a-vis the old *zaibatsu* was their lack of financial power, which derived from a lack of their own financial institutions. Nevertheless, this was precisely why backing was forthcoming from specialized banks, especially the Industrial Bank of Japan (IBJ). The government supported this role of the IBJ, raised the issuing ceiling of IBJ debentures from ¥500 million to ¥1 billion through the 1937 Provisional Funding Act, and also underwrote ¥350 million of the increase in the special fund account. Both the Deposit Bureau and the Bank of Japan also supplied the IBJ with funds through short-term lending and through a system of rediscounting, which resulted in a three-fold surge in outstanding loans from the IBJ to ¥1.16 billion in two short

---

[40]*Ibid.*, pp. 84-85.

[41]Morikawa, *Nihon Zaibatsushi, op. cit.,* p. 211.

years, as shown in Table 24. With government assistance, IBJ lending continued to grow after 1938, and in 1945 the Provisional Funding Act ultimately raised the ceiling on IBJ debenture issuing to ¥10 billion (Table 25).

TABLE 24

TOTAL LOANS AND OUTSTANDING AMOUNTS OF DEBENTURES BY INDUSTRIAL BANK OF JAPAN (THOUSAND YEN)

Year	Month	Loans	Debentures
1936	June	377,735	288,853
	Dec.	403,053	244,477
1937	June	438,981	244,968
	Dec.	826,493	640,867
1938	June	1,039,223	739,803
	Dec.	1,158,658	872,138
1939	June	1,080,984	880,961
	Dec.	1,366,489	865,520
1940	June	1,642,598	1,052,632
	Dec.	1,959,329	1,425,065

Source: Showa Zaiseishi XI, Finance II, edited by Ministry of Finance, *Toyo Keizai Shinposha*, 1957, p.115.

TABLE 25

ISSUANCE LIMITS OF DEBENTURES OF INDUSTRIAL BANK OF JAPAN (THOUSAND YEN)

Year	Month	Paid-in Capital	Limits of Insurance	
			IBJ ACT	Temporary Fund Adjustments Act
1937	September	35,000	35,000 * 10	500,000
1939	April	35,000	35,000 * 10	1,000,000
1939	August	87,500	87,500 * 10	1,000,000
1941	March	87,500	87,500 * 10	2,000,000
1942	March	87,500	87,500 * 10	5,000,000
1945	February	87,500	87,500 * 10	10,000,000

Source: Showa Zaiseishi XI, Finance II, *(op. cit.)*, p. 117.

Moreover, in order to meet the burgeoning demand for funds coming mainly from these newly risen concerns, joint financing was a frequent occurrence following the formation of a lending syndicate often lead-managed by the IBJ. In the period 1939-41, for example, of the 176 syndicate loans made, 118 were lead-managed by the IBJ, and new concerns such as Riken Kagaku, Nakajima Aviation, Toyota, and Nissan were major recipients. Although the underwriting syndicate for corporate issues had existed since Meiji times, this period saw its rapid expansion as a lending syndicate as well. It is also at this time that the framework for a central underwriting role by the IBJ was established. As will be discussed later, despite the post-war reforms, the financial system of the 1930s was kept virtually intact, and it is here that we find the original shape of the fund supplying patterns later used during the high growth period of the 1960s.

The arrangements that shaped the post-war financial system all came to the fore during this period--the highly centralized commercial banks, the postal saving system, and the *Nokyo* agricultural cooperatives (as well as the Deposit Bureau and its successor, the Trust Fund, both of which were supported by postal and pension funds), and an IBJ-dominated fund supplying method. Of course, the basic law that has regulated monetary policy throughout the post-war period, the Bank of Japan act, also has remained largely unchanged since its enactment in 1942.

As the greater part of the newly risen concerns' business bases were located in colonial areas, many were dissolved after the war. Yet some, like Nissan and Hitachi, which were later to be driving forces in Japan's burst of high growth, grew out of this group. For others, like Riken Kagaku and Nakajima Aviation, their technology and their technicians were to play a vital role in the post-war technical revolution, albeit in different organizations and in different ways. Apart from this more concrete legacy, the newly risen concerns also played an important role in the sense that they left behind them a corporate culture based on technology. According to Nakamura, "The shape of the newly risen concerns is closely resembled in the post-war era by Sony, National, Sanyo, Sharp, and more recently Pioneer--namely, all companies that owe their sudden rise to technological superiority."[42]

The "converted" *zaibatsu* also advanced rapidly through heavy industrialization and chemical engineering as they cooperated with the military. Mitsubishi, Mitsui, and Sumitomo all made especially fast progress in heavy industrialization. Table 26 compares the ratio of heavy and chemical industrialization on a paid-up capital basis for the years 1937 and 1945 for these three major *zaibatsu*. Each of them shows a jump from just under 50 percent to around 70 percent or almost 90 percent.

---

[42]Nakamura, *Showa Keizaishi, op. cit.,* p. 92.

TABLE 26

PAID-IN CAPITAL OF THREE MAJOR ZAIBATSU FIRMS (MILLIONS OF YEN)

| | | 1937 | | | 1945 | |
Industries	Mitsui	Mitsu-bishi	Sumi-tomo	Mitsui	Mitsu-bishi	Sumi-tomo
Heavy Industries						
Iron and Steel	162	106	34	481	274	111
Metal	15	12	56	270	185	530
Machinery	40	106	41	838	1,207	638
Shipbuilding	--	--	--	58	11	1
Chemical	80	36	38	566	`187	167
Subtotal	298	262	170	2,214	1,866	1,449
Light Industries	84	66	36	273	73	29
Finance	70	127	58	169	159	65
Other	159	118	121	403	604	102
Total	612	574	386	3,061	2,703	1,646

Source: Hidemasa Morikawa (1980), pp. 215-216.

Mitsubishi Heavy Industry and Sumitomo Metals were the leading stars of military-demand-dominated heavy and chemical industrialization. Mitsui also fostered Mitsui Zosen, Toyo Koatsu, and Mitsui Chemicals, but lagged considerably behind Mitsubishi and Sumitomo as a military-demand manufacturer. This rapid heavy and chemical industrialization of the old *zaibatsu* gave rise to an enormous demand for funds that could not be met by traditionally closed fund raising methods centering mainly on family connections. Coupled with the previously mentioned "conversion," this new situation quickly modified the closed nature of the old *zaibatsu* and was a major catalyst for significant organizational changes. In other words, the need for huge capital increases led to public stock offerings by the *zaibatsu*. This was followed in turn by the head companies also becoming stock companies and by the public sale of head company stock. The result of course was the collapse of the closed *zaibatsu* and the further strengthening of the professional managers vis-a-vis the *zaibatsu* families. The *zaibatsu* therefore suffered a substantial collapse even before they were "dissolved."

Another important factor in terms of the post-war economic systemic framework arguably was the enactment of provisional measures on imports and exports. These laws gave the Ministry of Trade, Commerce, and Industry--MITI's pre-war predecessor organization--broad powers concerning the production, distribution, consignment, use, and consumption of items of trade and trade products, and therefore provided a basis for initial post-war trade administration. Yet although control of trade by the MITI virtually ceased to exist when Japan became an IMF Article 8 country in the 1960s, these laws remain significant in terms of providing the starting point for the so-called administrative guidance wielded today.

In terms of power effects that are still apparent, the series of industrial laws enacted around 1935 were much more important. One archetypical example is the Oil Industry Act of 1934. At the time, the Japanese oil industry consisted of producing gasoline and heavy oil from imported crude oil. Instead of special protection for this most vital of military resources, the main purpose of this act was to introduce additional controls.

Spurred on by the Oil Industry Act, a whole series of laws were enacted, including the Automobile Production Industry Act and the Iron Manufacturing Industry Act (both in 1936), and the Machine Tools Act and the Aircraft Manufacturing Industry Act (both in 1938). Industries were organized along the lines established by these laws, and the industrial associations set up to represent the various industries were then used as channels for administrative guidance or for conveying private industry views to the public sector. It is from this period, therefore, that the current pattern of Japanese government policy measures would seem to stem. Naturally, the relative positions of power between the government and the companies that stare at each other across the buffering zone of their industrial associations have greatly changed since the pre-war era. Nevertheless, the enactment of industrial laws at that time was extremely important. It established a framework for the consistent formation of what MIT economist Richard J. Samuels calls "mutual understanding."[43]

Historical Changes in Japanese Public Works

It was shown in Chapter 2 that public-sector activity in Japan has largely revolved around public works carried out on a local government basis. It can also be said that the political and administrative framework surrounding these public-works bodies has existed since Meiji times. Table 27 gives a breakdown of gross government and private sector domestic capital formation in Japan since Meiji. With the exception of the World War I period (1916-20) and the immediate pre-World War II years (1936-40), the share of government non-military capital formation was extremely large--always within the 25-40 percent range--and was especially high during the depression. Although the share has fallen somewhat in

---

[43]Richard J. Samuels, "Nihon ni Okeru Kokka no Business," *Leviathan,* Spring, 1988.

TABLE 27

GOVERNMENT CAPITAL FORMATION AND GROSS DOMESTIC CAPITAL FORMATION (MILLIONS OF YEN)

| | Government Capital Formation | | | Gross Domestic Capital Formation | | (1)/(4) | GCF/GDCF (%) | |
	Including Military (1)	Non-military (2)	Adjustment of (2), (3)	Including Military (4)	Non-military (5)	=(6)	(2)/(5) =(7)	(3)/(5) =(8)
1887-1896	38	30	22	119	111	31.7	25.0	19.8
1892-1901	91	69	52	195	173	46.7	35.6	30.1
1897-1906	135	104	73	261	230	51.6	39.6	31.7
1902-1911	196	163	122	390	357	50.2	41.8	34.2
1907-1916	266	226	169	537	497	49.5	42.0	34.0
1912-1921	546	423	309	1,290	1,166	42.3	32.7	26.5
1917-1926	985	714	618	2,253	1,982	43.7	31.6	31.2
1922-1931	1,151	1,043	767	2,440	2,332	47.1	42.7	32.9
1927-1936	1,257	1,092	704	2,596	2,431	48.4	42.0	29.0
1931-1940	2,478	1,333	812	5,128	3,983	48.3	26.0	20.4
1951-1955*	--	572	--	--	1,836	--	31.1	--
1956-1960*	--	985	--	--	3,789	--	25.9	--

Source: Columns (1), (2), (4), and (5) of periods 1887-1940 are from Ohkawa and Rosovsky (1973),   pp. 2, 9.

* From "Economic White Paper," Economic Planning Agency, 1963.

the post-war era, it has maintained at a level of 25-30 percent--as was shown in Chapter 2, a comparatively high advantage.

Table 28 depicts how large a share so-called infrastructure investment (in railways, roads, ports, waterways, forestry conservation, agriculture and fisheries, and telegraph and telephone systems) accounted for in total government non-military fixed-capital formation. As is clear from the table, infrastructure investment has accounted for the lion's share of government fixed-capital investment since Meiji times, with public transport- and telecommunications-related investment recording especially significant growth.

TABLE 28

GOVERNMENT FIXED-CAPITAL FORMATION (NOMINAL), FISCAL 1870-1965 (MILLIONS OF YEN)

Fiscal Year	Rivers	Railways	Roads	Ports	Agriculture and Fishery	Forestry	Tele-communications	Total
1877	1.865	.030	1.107	.006	.264	--	--	3.272
1887	4.462	11.307	4.231	.169	.401	--	--	20.570
1897	20.208	38.983	11.108	.504	.464	--	2.402	73.669
1907	16.104	24.306	25.218	5.759	2.713	--	3.663	77.761
1917	19.362	57.491	22.263	5.150	4.686	.242	8.453	117.647
1920	72.182	171.570	76.043	17.524	10.880	.879	40.720	389.788
1923	67.934	192.105	124.752	38.828	18.263	1.580	27.953	459.415
1924	59.008	196.151	130.391	24.708	18.987	1.637	18.342	449.224
1925	50.218	198.249	147.763	22.083	17.439	1.828	34.859	472.439
1926	59.473	207.329	154.305	23.818	21.925	2.058	51.305	520.211
1927	64.964	218.480	165.814	27.305	26.635	2.428	48.685	554.311
1928	64.609	212.581	184.511	25.098	31.839	2.671	36.939	558.248
1929	58.137	199.120	179.778	24.969	32.830	2.866	39.114	536.814
1930	48.173	116.641	149.278	24.518	33.274	2.302	20.940	395.126
1931	45.038	95.000	161.441	24.828	27.977	2.317	12.292	368.893
1932	71.912	102.400	211.100	34.231	58.876	4.684	23.113	506.316
1933	78.712	121.600	183.309	43.875	78.908	7.173	24.804	536.381
1934	70.670	130.900	161.989	36.103	70.045	6.473	25.238	501.418
1935	76.802	88.800	182.093	36.219	44.350	7.712	39.936	475.912
1936	85.030	151.800	223.221	39.630	44.601	6.914	40.808	592.004
1937	90.598	169.400	161.897	36.822	48.931	10.063	62.137	579.848
1938	92.459	181.700	185.327	35.108	50.621	10.221	44.435	599.871

(Continued)

TABLE 28

GOVERNMENT FIXED-CAPITAL FORMATION (NOMINAL), FISCAL 1870-1965 (MILLIONS OF YEN)

Fiscal Year	Rivers	Railways	Roads	Ports	Agriculture and Fishery	Forestry	Tele-communications	Total
1939	113.685	227.200	149.792	39.528	75.438	12.190	37.571	579.848
1940	119.122	287.100	169.588	44.122	88.598	11.993	38.295	734.818
1941	150.571	296.200	173.082	55.679	122.583	11.896	38.628	838.637
1942	167.360	302.300	175.977	73.677	131.351	11.807	35.536	898.000
1943	170.510	583.700	178.819	82.761	221.624	12.317	85.669	1,335.400
1944	184.845	831.100	194.028	107.194	507.043	13.459	103.082	1,940.779
1945	217.000	686.000	209.000	75.000	1,365.000	14.000	186.000	2,758.000
1946	806.000	3,756.000	2,454.000	243.000	2,399.000	141.000	1,368.000	11,178.000
1947	2,916.000	8,582.000	3,230.000	814.000	5,671.000	319.000	5,148.000	28,720.000
1948	11,521.000	20,951.000	8,540.000	5,423.000	17,610.000	1,499.000	13,0867.000	78,613.000
1949	25,188.000	16,163.000	20,765.000	7,022.000	20,952.000	1,968.000	14,307.000	108,336.000
1950	45,449.000	24,364.000	33,219.000	7,644.000	35,520.000	3,755.000	19,108.000	169,060.000
1951	46,567.000	38,734.000	36,764.000	8,714.000	44,855.000	6,488.000	29,141.000	211,261.000
1952	57,171.000	44,165.000	57,880.000	11,829.000	64,973.000	7,631.000	30,233.000	273,883.000
1953	69,316.000	54,637.000	65,268.000	15,688.000	85,579.000	9,464.000	58,771.000	358,722.000
1954	63,657.000	51,824.000	68,842.000	11,863.000	75,511.000	9,176.000	50,375.000	331,249.000
1955	60,456.000	52,008.000	82,920.000	11,510.000	70,797.000	8,937.000	52,291.000	338,920.000
1956	49,158.000	58,033.000	92,696.000	13,178.000	71,135.000	8,224.000	65,399.000	358,041.000
1957	60,460.000	97,009.000	130,544.000	17,345.000	77,648.000	8,180.000	88,801.000	459,788.000
1958	67,912.000	85,163.000	153,345.000	20,602.000	84,430.000	8,947.000	80,414.000	500,814.000
1959	91,008.000	104,518.000	188,968.000	28,286.000	98,892.000	11,287.000	97,824.000	820,761.000
1960	117,895.000	110,814.000	213,911.000	34,132.000	116,856.000	12,504.000	133,260.000	739,372.000

(Continued)

TABLE 28

GOVERNMENT FIXED-CAPITAL FORMATION (NOMINAL), FISCAL 1870-1965 (MILLIONS OF YEN)

Fiscal Year	Rivers	Railways	Roads	Ports	Agriculture and Fishery	Forestry	Tele-communications	Total
1961	130,105.000	177,073.000	313,204.000	41,909.000	139,559.000	15,178.000	172,307.000	989,335.000
1962	136,323.000	226,855.000	385,436.000	51,902.000	155,711.000	16,985.000	206,540.000	1,179,752.000
1963	157,777.000	277,594.000	446,856.000	58,224.000	166,418.000	20,062.000	246,482.000	1,373,413.000
1964	169,301.000	257,126.000	513,831.000	63,792.000	189,864.000	23,160.000	283,300.000	1,500,374.000
1965	219,131.000	328,671.000	538,244.000	84,203.000	225,767.000	28,585.000	346,300.000	1,770,701.000

Sources: Moriyuki Sawamoto, *op. cit.,* 1981, pp. 278-79 and "Seifu Kotei shihon Keisei oyobi Seifu Shihon Stock no Suikei," Economic Planning Agency, May, 1968.

Whereas waterways works accounted for the greater part around 1877, national railway investment jumped during the latter half of the Meiji period, with a network of lines being virtually completed by around 1907. Elsewhere, investment in roads began to account for a larger share of infrastructure investment starting around 1920 with the enactment of the Road Act. Under the aforementioned Takahashi fiscal policy, moreover, road investment played an important part in the regional and rural Opportune Assistance Program, and therefore grew substantially.

Agriculture, fisheries, and forestry accounted for only a minimal share for most of the Meiji and Taisho periods (1868-1925), but received a major boost under the Hara-Takahashi government and its concerted fiscal program of regional and rural assistance. This share went on to grow further in the post-war period, first to counter acute food shortages and later to boost food production. Although the share has since dropped, such investment remains an important facet of public works even today.

In general terms, public transport and telecommunications infrastructure-- including rail, road, telegraph, and telephones--has been a major pillar of central government or public corporation activity since the Meiji period.

TABLE 29

INVESTMENTS IN TRANSPORTATION AND TELECOMMUNICATION FACILITIES (FISCAL YEARS 1870-1964, FIVE-YEAR AVERAGE PRICES ADJUSTED BY 1960 PRICE)

Fiscal Year	Transportation and Telecommunications Investment (A)	GNP (B)	Government Fixed-capital Formation (C)	Total Infrastructure Investment (D)	(A)/(B)	(A)/(C)	(A)/(D)	(D)/(C)
1870-74	6.39	--	11.52	7.47	--	55.4	85.5	64.8
1875-79	3.17	--	15.18	7.89	--	20.9	40.2	52.0
1880-84	13.06	817.5	31.98	21.13	1.6	40.8	61.8	66.1
1885-89	22.17	983.5	38.96	30.55	2.3	56.9	72.6	78.4
1890-94	30.85	1,230.6	52.09	42.41	2.5	59.2	72.7	81.4
1895-99	40.86	1,483.7	74.12	57.52	2.8	55.1	71.0	77.6
1900-04	50.60	1,697.4	94.41	64.32	3.0	53.6	78.7	68.1
1905-09	41.76	1,908.4	101.63	55.95	2.2	41.1	74.6	55.1
1910-14	67.33	2,340.8	146.30	91.61	2.9	46.0	73.5	62.6
1915-19	44.01	3,123.2	103.17	60.97	1.4	42.7	72.2	59.1
1920-24	98.11	3,417.3	219.71	121.99	2.9	44.7	80.4	55.5
1925-29	139.90	4,404.0	322.01	167.25	3.2	43.4	83.6	51.9
1930-34	145.88	5,080.0	341.24	197.70	2.9	42.7	73.8	57.9
1935-39	151.03	6,837.5	352.02	204.31	2.2	42.9	73.9	58.0
1940-44	130.60	7,270.6	287.36	193.04	1.8	45.4	67.7	67.2
1945-49	119.72	4,460.2	483.94	194.71	2.7	24.7	61.5	40.2
1950-54	188.87	7,026.3	629.47	387.96	2.7	30.0	48.7	61.6
1955-59	319.82	10,510.3	859.99	493.76	3.0	37.2	64.8	57.4
1960-64	748.83	18,266.4	1,830.61	1,005.86	4.1	40.9	74.4	54.9

Source: Moriyuki Sawamoto, "Kokyo Toshi Hyakunen no Ayumi, Nihon Keizai no Hatten to Tomoni" (Taisei Shupan, 1981) p. 22.

The Meiji position that "all roads be nationally built" has been altered slightly with the introduction after World War II of a system of prefectural and municipal roads. Yet rural works began to expand significantly with the start of the Showa period (1926), which in turn led to a gradual increase in the profile of local government as a contractor of public works.

The regional share, which jumped in the later half of the 1920s, fell at one stage due to burgeoning military expenses accompanying World War II and to the chaos of the post-war period. Yet it recovered steadily thereafter and stabilized at around just over 60 percent, an even higher level than in early Showa. After the war, however, the prefectural share (even excluding that of Tokyo) came to account for a larger share than in pre-war days.

CHART 6

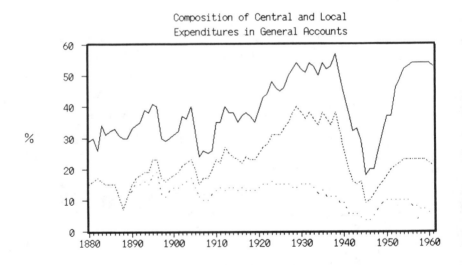

Composition of Central and Local
Expenditures in General Accounts

Under Prime Minister Yasuhiro Nakasone, both the national railway and state telecommunications company were privatized, cutting drastically the level of direct infrastructure investment witnessed in Japan since Meiji. In comparison to the pre-war period, however, the regional share of roads, agriculture, forestry and fishery, ports, forestry conservation, and so on has been preserved and expanded to such an extent that they now form the core of the current public sector, as has been explained in Chapter 2.

Farmland Reform and Japanese Agriculture

One prominent feature of Japanese agriculture since the Meiji period seems to be its failure to achieve in any consistent way its goal of "capitalistic agricultural production," or large-scale production. Moreover, hardly any changes have taken place in the basic production pattern of agriculture, especially from Meiji to 1955-1965. During this period according to agricultural economist Minoru Haneda, "the agricultural population numbered 14 million, farm households 5.5 million, and land under cultivation 6 million hectares . . . ."[44] Moreover, the average statistic of one hectare under cultivation per farm household remains unchanged even when post-1965 figures are counted.

---

[44]Minoru Haneda, *Nihon Nogyo no Henbo-Nogyo Kozo Mondai Nyumon* (Nogyo Shinko Chiiki Chosakai, November, 1985).

TABLE 30

STRUCTURE OF JAPANESE AGRICULTURE

Year	Cultivated Areas (1,000 Hectares)	Cultivated Areas per Agriculture Household (Hectares)	Total Population (10,000)	Total Labor Force (10,000)	Total Agricultural Labor Force (10,000 & %)	Agricultural Household (1,000)	Agricultural Household Specialized in Agriculture (1,000 & %)	Agricultural Household not Specialized in Agriculture (1,000 & %)
1904	5,251	0.97	4,614	2,602	1,567	5,417	3,777	1,640(30.3)
1906	5,293	0.98	4,704	2,633	1,573	5,378	3,810	1,584(29.2)
1908	5,459	1.01	4,797	2,660	1,592	5,408	3,748	1,662(30.7)
1910	5,606	1.03	4,918	2,692	1,571	5,417	3,695	1,722(31.8)
1915	5,811	1.07	5,275	2,723	1,495	5,451	3,748	1,703(31.2)
1919	6,021	1.10	5,503	2,736	1,394	5,481	3,837	1,644(29.3)
1920	6,034	1.10	5,547	2,737	1,373	5,485	3,823	1,662(30.3)
1925	6,017	1.08	5,974	2,844	1,332	5,549	3,880	1,668(30.1)
1930	5,867	1.05	6,445	2,962	1,374	5,600	4,042	1,558(27.8)
1935	6,008	1.07	6,925	3,140	1,336	5,611	4,164	1,447(25.8)
1940	6,027	--	7,193	3,248	1,336	--	--	--
1941	5,812	1.06	7,222	3,258	1,362	5,499	2,304	3,195(58.1)
1947	5,242	0.89	7,810	3,333	1,662	5,909	3,275	2,635(44.6)
1950	5,048	0.82	8,320	3,563	1,610	6,176	3,086	3,090(50.0)
1955	5,140	0.86	8,928	4,122	1,470	6,043	2,105	3,983(65.2)
1960	6,071	0.88	9,342	4,465	1,196	6,057	2,078	3,979(65.7)
1965	6,004	0.91	9,828	4,754	981	5,665	1,291	4,446(78.5)
1970	5,796	0.96	10,372	5,109	811	5,402	845	4,557(84.4)
1975	5,572	0.97	11,194	5,240	588	4,953	616	4,337(87.6)
1980	6,461	1.01	11,706	5,664	506	4,661	623	4,038(86.6)
1985	5,379	1.07	12,024	5,766	468	4,376	626	3,750(85.7)

(Continued)

TABLE 30

STRUCTURE OF JAPANESE AGRICULTURE

Agricultural Household not Specialized in Agriculture Category I (1,000 & %)	Agricultural Household not Specialized in Agriculture Category II (1,000 & %)
2040(37.1)	1,155(21.0)
1684(28.5)	951(16.1)
1753(28.4)	1,337(21.6)
2275(37.6)	1,663(27.5)
2036(33.6)	1,942(32.1)
2081(36.7)	2,365(41.8)
1814(33.6)	2,743(50.8)
1259(25.4)	3,078(67.1)
1002(21.5)	3,036(65.1)
775(17.7)	2,975(67.9)

Source: Minoru Hata, "Nihon Nogyo no Henbo--Nogyo Kozo Mondai Nyumon" (Nogyo Shinko Chiiki Chosakai, 1985) pp.. 22-23.

These trends contrast directly with the British case, where "farmland reform" was realized after the first and second enclosures, and was followed by capitalistic agricultural production. Of course, agricultural problems take on varied forms in the process of capitalist development. Yet even compared to France, for example, where relatively small farmers have been strong historically, the area of land cultivated by the Japanese farmer is extremely small. As Table 31 clearly shows, whereas the average land area cultivated by the French farmer in 1980 was 16.7 hectares, the corresponding Japanese figure was a tiny 1.07 hectares.

TABLE 31

POPULATION OF EC COUNTRIES AND THEIR AGRICULTURAL INDICES

Country	Population (Millions)	Cultivated Areas (1,000 Hectares)	Numbers of Agricultural Households (1,000)	Agricultural Labor Force (1,000)	Rate of Reduction of the ALF (%)	Export/Import Ratio of Agricultural Products (%)	Ratio of Agricultural Labor Force to Total (%)	Ratio of Agricultural Income to Total (%)
West Germany	61.6	7,495	797	1,436	29.3	43	6.0	2.2
Italy	57.1	12,753	2,192	2,925	22.7	43	14.2	6.4
United Kingdom	56.0	7,013	249	643	11.5	49	2.7	2.0
France	53.7	18,962	1,135	1,841	30.4	125	8.8	4.2
Spain	37.4	20,500	1,939	2,122	34.2	88	18.9	7.1
Netherlands	14.2	869	129	247	13.1	139	6.0	--
Belgium	9.9	781	91	112	30.9	76	3.0	2.1
Portugal	9.9	3,670	--	1,120	--	44	28.5	--
Greece	9.6	3,909	734	1,016	21.3	143	28.5	15.5
Denmark	5.1	2,650	116	176	20.3	244	8.1	4.5
Ireland	3.4	1,248	225	212	19.7	228	19.2	12.8
Luxembourg	0.4	59	5	9	28.3	76	5.7	2.5
Japan	116.8	5,461	4,662	5,770	29.5	10	10.4	3.8

Sources: Osamu Yamamoto, ed., "Nogyo Kaikaku no Tenkai to Genjyo" (Ienohikari Kyokai, 1988).
Data are from "Review of Agricultural Policies in OECD Member Countries," 1980-1982, OECD, p. 143.

Nevertheless, it would be inaccurate to say that no change has taken place in Japanese agriculture since the Meiji period. Recall the aforementioned move from tenant farmer to independent farmer, the establishment of owner agriculture in the late 1920s and its culmination in farmland reform, and the sharp drop in the farming population from 1955 as Japan entered its high growth phase. Haneda argues the following point:

> So after virtually no change from Meiji until 1955-65, the agricultural labor force started to plunge. It fell to some 4.5 million, or one-third of what it was. Agricultural surveys have further shown that of those whose principal place of employ is agriculture, those under 60 years of age have fallen from 9.98 million in 1960 to 2.74 million in 1984, or a decrease of 27.5 percent . . . . The "ratio of people to land" or the amount of land under cultivation per farmer has therefore changed substantially, but the striking change in the nature of the 4.38 million farming households is also an extremely important change . . . . [This is part of] a trend first, where farming households are beginning to split up into those enthusiastically engaged in agriculture (the professional farmer) and those who work elsewhere (the part-time farmer), and second, where the professional farmers are beginning to split up into those farming large tracts of land for crops like wheat, or dairy farming, and those farming smaller tracts of market gardening, or chicken or pig breeding. This division into two distinct groups lies at the very heart of the *Transfiguration of Japanese Agriculture.*"[45]

The Fundamentals of Agriculture Act (1961), which was enacted in response to Haneda's *Transfiguration of Japanese Agriculture*, was a major catalyst in shifting the Ministry of Agriculture and Fisheries' policies towards the modernization and rationalization of agriculture as an industry. Some 261 agricultural ordinances aimed at the structural reform of agricultural administration and the preparation of a new, overall framework were enacted between 1960 and 1986. Much controversy exists concerning whether agricultural administration since the Fundamentals of Agriculture Act should be seen as a complete departure from past patterns or whether it represents adjustment within the independent-farmer framework.[46] Irrespective of this duality, however, several aspects of the

---

[45]*Ibid.*

[46]Kunio Takenaka and Hisanori Nishiyama take a Marxist approach in *Nogyo Seisaku to Nogyo Hosei-Sengo Nosei no Tenkai to Nogyo Kankeiho* (Gakuyo Shobo, 1985), and interpret the enactment of the Fundamentals of Agriculture Act, as well as the 1970 Agricultural Land Act and the 1981 amendment of the three

Act prevent it from being seen as a bold policy change from the basic early-Showa structure of agriculture.[47] Let us consider this point in the context of changes that have been made in the Agricultural Land Act and the Staple Food Control Act, both of which regulate the basic structure of Japanese agricultural administration.

It is an accepted fact today that the farmland reform that took place immediately after World War II was the "skillful result of a wedding of internal forces encouraging such reform and foreign pressure in the form of the occupation."[48] Kenzo Matsumura, Minister of Agriculture and Forestry in the Shidehara Cabinet, believed that drastic reform was called for in the light of the social attitudes and food conditions at that time. And in fact, the initial proposal for farmland reform that the Japanese government put forward was bitterly opposed by groups representing landlord interests, and could not have become legislation without the support of the occupation forces. Later, a second reform bill stemming from an occupation force initiative did become law, but it is obvious that the first proposal was the heir of pre-war reform trends. Efforts to build up independent farmers had been making steady progress within the Japanese government--the implementation of the 1924 Tenant Farmer Mediation Act, the 1938 Farmland Adjustment Act, and the 1944 subsidy system for establishing independent farmers. A total of 2.766 million hectares was made available by these reforms by 1951--1.782 million hectares of farmland, 374,000 hectares of pasturage, and 610,000 hectares of uncultivated land. This very thorough reform placed 90 percent of Japanese agricultural land under independent farmers.

This unification of farmland ownership and management coupled with the dissolution of the *zaibatsu* determined the fundamental shape of the Japanese

---

agricultural land acts, as signaling the end of the doctrine of the independent farmer.

[47]"On the one hand, this law applied economic rationality to agriculture and aimed at expanding advantageous areas in terms of price structure as well as improving productivity. On the other, in order to rectify the disparity between agricultural and non-agricultural income, the law mandated price stability for agricultural output and demonstrated a direct protective stance. It was as if one arm was trying to shift away from the previous method of agricultural administration while the other was trying to maintain it. This stance survives even today and remains the basic undertone of agricultural administration." Nakamura, *Nihonkeizai-Sono Seicho to Kozo, op. cit,* p. 328.

[48]Keiki Owada, *Hishi Nihon no Nochi Kaikaku-Nosei Tantosha no Kaiso,* (Nihon Keizai Shinbunsha, 1981).

economy, which revolved around employee sovereignty and the doctrine of the independent farmer. The elimination of the capitalists, however, gave birth to a new rising force in secondary and tertiary industry--the so-called "third-class executive." This development led to the revival of the private sector and of the large corporation through manager leadership. Yet, as will be discussed later, the public aspects of agricultural operations become increasingly strong, especially with price controls and the organization of agricultural cooperatives. The first clause of the Agricultural Land Act (1952), which deals with farmland reform in aggregate, extols the doctrine of the independent farmer and states that it "recognizes that farmland is best owned by the actual cultivator, protecting his rights, and coordinating the use of land as farmland, thereby endeavoring to stabilize the position of the cultivator and to raise agricultural productivity." Although a later amendment has been made concerning collective usage, the unification of ownership and management--in other words the basic principle of fostering the independent farmer--remains unchanged.[49]

The Staple Food Control Act, enacted in 1942, was also born of this doctrine of the independent farmer. That is to say, the power of the landlord was greatly curtailed by both the state control of rice--including rice rents--and by the shift (from a system of farm rent paid in-kind to one of money payment). Specifically, on the one hand, the government effectively keep farm rents low by keeping its rice buying price low at ¥550 per *koku* (5.119 U.S. bushels), and on the other, it paid increased output subsidies to purchase from producers--but not from landlords. By 1945, the initial increased output subsidy of ¥5 per *koku* had risen to ¥245, accounting for a huge 82 percent of the producers' rice price per *koku* of ¥300. Plainly, the demise of the tenant farming system brought on by the Staple Food Control Act was a precursor to post-war farmland reform.

As is the case with the Agricultural Land Act, the Staple Food Control Act gradually took shape from early Showa and can be traced to the Rice Act of 1921, which was a response to rice riots. After an amendment in 1931, the same act led to the Rice Control Act of 1933. Despite its name, this act did not mandate any direct control, but left the distribution of rice up to free-market mechanisms. The government merely played the role of market price stabilizer by purchasing within a fixed price range.

Later, during World War II, the Staple Food Control Act was enacted. It represented a shift from indirect to direct control. During the post-war food crisis,

---

[49]". . . protecting his rights, and coordinating the use of land in order to promote the efficient use of land as farmland, thereby endeavoring . . .," Clause 1, 1970 Amended Act.

however, this direct control was implemented in the most extreme form--coerced supply. Once greater economic stability was restored, the emphasis of the Staple Food Control Act gradually changed from procuring food to securing income for rice farmers. For instance, the method for determining rice prices was also changed in 1952, from a price parity method to an income parity method. It was changed again in 1960 to a method of production-cost income supplementation. Under this approach, rice prices were made to conform with urban wages, which had started to escalate as the economy took off and a labor shortage emerged. This policy led to an almost four-fold increase in rice prices between 1960 and 1975. Since then, several modifications have been made, including a shift from a "rationing system" to a "distribution system" with the introduction of the quality differentiation system (1979) and the Amended Staple Food Act (1981), the clarification of the legal status of independent rice distribution, and the allowing of the trading of gift rice, etc. Nevertheless, the larger framework of government management of all rice, including independently distributed rice, remains untouched.

Therefore, it was within the bounds of the Agricultural Land Act and the Staple Food Act, not by any far-reaching policy changes in the basic structure of agriculture, that the former agricultural administration tried to modernize and rationalize agricultural output. The "agricultural transfiguration" Haneda speaks of has been brought about by the response of the agricultural sector and rural village themselves to a different economic environment.

High growth throughout the economy brought rapid technological progress to the agricultural sector as well, and agricultural output was greatly improved by mechanization, better quality, the development of new fertilizers, and new pesticides and weed killers. Table 32 is a comparison of changes in agricultural labor output and changes in manufacturing output between 1960 and 1985. It shows agriculture outstripping manufacturing.

TABLE 32

LABOR PRODUCTIVITY OF AGRICULTURE AND MANUFACTURING

Fiscal Year	Production Index		Labor Force Index		Labor Productivity Index	
	Agriculture	Manufacturing	Agriculture	Manufacturing	Agriculture	Manufacturing
1960	76.9	19.2	236.4	69.9	32.5	27.5
1965	85.9	32.5	193.9	85.2	44.3	38.1
1973	98.2	85.8	123.7	105.5	79.4	81.3
1979	107.7	97.9	107.3	98.4	100.4	99.5
1981	102.0	102.0	96.4	101.1	105.8	100.9
1982	104.1	101.4	95.5	101.0	109.0	100.4
1983	104.8	108.0	91.5	102.8	114.5	105.1
1984	109.8	118.8	89.5	105.5	122.7	112.6
1985	110.8	122.8	87.7	106.1	126.3	115.7
Rate of growth over previous year (%)						
1960-65	2.2	11.1	-3.9	4.0	6.4	6.7
1965-73	1.7	12.9	-5.5	2.7	7.6	9.9
1973-79	1.6	2.2	-2.3	-1.2	4.0	3.4
1979-81	-2.7	2.1	-5.2	1.4	2.7	0.7
1982	2.1	-0.6	-0.9	-0.1	3.0	-0.5
1983	0.7	6.5	-4.2	1.8	5.0	4.7
1984	4.8	10.0	-2.2	2.6	7.2	7.1
1985	0.9	3.4	-2.0	0.6	2.9	2.8

Source: "Zusetsu Nogyo Hakusho, Fiscal 1986" (Norin Tokei Kyokai, 1987) p. 28

This improvement in productivity meant that agriculture no longer needed the huge seasonal labor inputs of earlier days. The sector's response has the been aforementioned split into full-time and part-time farming. It is certainly valid economically to attempt to bolster "structural reform" towards full-time farming in order to secure "agriculture's position as an industry." But as Nakamura says, greater part-time farming is the result of rational behavior that "compares the scale and profitability of farm management with non-farm profitability" and "holds on to an asset while generating some rice and a small amount cash revenue at the same time."[50] Therefore, it will be no easy task to persuade farmers to give up agricultural land if the current structure of agricultural administration is left as is. For Nakamura, this means that "the current shape is only made rational by the continued presence of significant government protectionist policies, and agriculture as we know it today will continue to exist as long as these policies remain unchanged."

This is quite clear from Table 33. It shows that living standards for farmers since 1972 have surpassed those of worker households. The main reason is that households of Type 2 part-time farmers have a much higher standard of living than worker households. Another revealing perspective on this discrepancy: In fiscal 1985, although household accounts for Type 2 part-time farmers were 16.3 percent higher than those of worker households, accounts for full-time farmers were 12.2 percent lower than those of worker households. Although it may not necessarily be correct to assume that people act according to economic rationality alone, when an income gap this wide exists between full-time and part-time farming, it seems only natural to choose part-time farming, and Type 2 part-time farming at that.

---

[50]Nakamura, *Nihon Keizai-Sono Seicho to Kozo, op. cit.,* p. 333.

TABLE 33

COMPARISON OF HOUSEHOLD INCOME OF AGRICULTURE VERSUS COMPANY EMPLOYEES (PER CAPITA)

Fiscal Year	Household Income of Agriculture (1,000 ¥)	Employees Household of the Country=100	Ratio to Employees Household		
			Employee Households of Cities of Various Sizes=100		
			Cities of Population Above 50,000	Cities of Population Below 50,000	Towns and Villages
All agricultural households					
1960	60.7	75.9	70.8	--	--
1965	115.5	82.7	78.4	94.9	97.1
1970	236.8	95.3	92.6	103.5	103.4
1975	546.4	107.1	106.4	109.1	108.1
1983	916.9	110.6	108.6	117.3	117.2
1984	957.7	111.4	109.4	117.9	118.3
1985	980.6	112.2	110.1	118.9	118.7
Agricultural households specialized in agriculture (with primary male workers)					
1984	752.2	87.5	85.9	92.6	92.9
1985	767.4	87.8	86.2	93.1	92.9
Agricultural households not specialized in agriculture category I (temporary outside jobs)					
1984	795.7	92.6	90.9	89.0	98.3
1985	763.2	87.3	85.7	92.6	92.4
Agricultural households not specialized in agriculture category II (permanent outside jobs)					
1984	1,000	116.3	114.2	123.1	123.5
1985	1,017	116.3	114.2	123.3	123.1

Source:　"Zusetsu Nogyo Hakusho, Fiscal 1986" (Norin Tokei Kyokai, 1987) p. 28.

BEYOND CAPITALISM

Chapter 1 argued that employee sovereignty in the private sector established by the break-up of the *zaibatsu* and the doctrine of owner-farmers completed by agricultural land reform have been the main determinants of the fundamental nature of the Japanese economy in the Showa period. Yet the agricultural sector's price control and regulation of distribution, stemming from the Staple Food Act, contrast sharply with the fierce competition in the markets of the large corporate sector. The price and distribution system in this agricultural sector smacks more of a planned economy than a market economy. Of course, in the many cases already mentioned, the planning authority is the cooperative or local government, and regulated prices for agricultural produce--including rice, farmer income, and production plans--are determined not in the final analysis by the market but by politics. Therefore, the development of agriculture as an industry has been significantly limited.

The evolution of Showa agricultural policy based on the principle of owner-farmers brought about both a marked levelling of income and the elevation of the rural populace into the middle class--to the point where farmer income exceeded worker income. Elsewhere, however, it gave rise to a large volume of "landed" part-time cultivators, and it is gradually sapping the vitality of the agricultural community.

Dissolution of the *Zaibatsu* and Post-war Reconstruction

The Imperial proclamation of defeat was made on August 15, 1945, but because of our very thorough trading information network at headquarters, we at Mitsui knew that things weren't going Japan's way. Still, it wasn't clear if we'd be able to overcome military resistance and actually end the war. So we were quite relieved to hear the proclamation. At the same time, I also felt that this time it was Mitsui's turn. Right from the time of the Manchurian Incident, Mitsui had been labelled pacifist or liberalist or pro-American, and was disapproved of--especially by military right-wingers. In terms of business, we had been shut out of Manchuria and Northern China and come under various kinds of pressure, which had let the other *zaibatsu* catch up with us. We were fairly naive in believing that this time it was our turn, that the peace industries which would put the country back on its feet were where we excelled, that the United Kingdom and the United States wouldn't act unfavorably towards us, that everything was going to get better.

Hideo Edo, Yoshio Ando (ed.),
Showa Keizaishi e no Shogen
(Mainichi Shimbunsha, 1966)

In fact, the so-called old *zaibatsu* such as Mitsui felt they had suffered most from the military campaign against the entire *zaibatsu* establishment, and as such, they expected favorable treatment from the occupation forces. Mitsui, for example, defended itself by quoting the Shansi incidents, which helped fuel the Sino-Japanese conflict. (Having provoked the military, Mitsui was expelled from Shansi province and all its directors, from the chairman down, were forced to resign.) The then foreign minister, Shigeru Yoshida, also came to Mitsui's defence, saying that although he did now know the new ones, the old *zaibatsu* were "good *zaibatsu*."

Yet economist Calvin Edwards of the occupation forces, author of the 1946 Edwards Report--which essentially sought the dissolution of the *zaibatsu* and the eradication of concentrated economic power--believed that the *zaibatsu*, along with the military, were intrinsically responsible for Japan's strategy of aggression. He also viewed them as the largest obstacle to the democratization of Japan. Edwards' view on the Japanese economy closely resembled that of the Koza School of Marxism, which argued that *zaibatsu* families' feudalistic control led to export dependence and external aggression by suppressing wages and thus continually constricting the domestic market. Dissolution of the *zaibatsu* was imperative for the democratization of Japan. Further, not only Edwards but a great many GHQ staff at the time had been involved in the anti-trust measures formulated in the latter part of the American New Deal. In light of a world-wide tide against monopolies, they were very firmly opposed to the Japanese *zaibatsu*.

To take an extreme view, occupation policies in Japan acted as a kind of laboratory for U.S. antitrust theory.[51] As a result, *zaibatsu* dissolution in Japan was extremely thorough. The head offices of eleven *zaibatsu*, including Mitsui, Mitsubishi, Sumitomo, and Yasuda, were dissolved, with the *zaibatsu* families, even those still legally minors, all being purged. This process was so thorough that when Mitsui Bussan and Mitsubishi Shoji were dissolved in 1947, any two or more employees from these two companies were prohibited from setting up companies together. According to Hideo Edo, former chairman of Mitsui Real Estate, "As one of the victims caught in the middle, I may be a little subjective, but the policies that American and the occupation forces took were too severe. We were treated like war criminals. The worst was how they treated the *zaibatsu* families. What happened to their assets was worse than a war crime."[52]

---

[51]Antitrust policy in late New Deal America was pursued by the Temporary National Economic Council (TNEC), of which GHQ Civilian Affairs Bureau deputy chief Charles L. Kades and antitrust/cartel chairman Edward C. Welsh were members.

[52]Edo, *Showa Keizaishi e no Shogen, op. cit.*

Edo, however, goes on to discuss in an overall way the impact of *zaibatsu* dissolution as follows:

I believe that such drastic measures as dissolving the *zaibatsu,* appropriating 90 percent of their assets, and freeing up agricultural land in the end squashed the chances for social revolution growing amongst the defeated Japanese masses. Japan was able to rise up from its terrible economic debilitation, recover from the ravages of war, and carry out an economic leap such as the world had yet to witness partly because the dissolution of the *zaibatsu,* which controlled every sector of the Japanese economy before the war, allowed individual companies with fresh, new management to line up at the same start line and participate enthusiastically in free competition. To be frank, I would have to admit that the dissolution of the *zaibatsu* did create greater economic democracy.[53]

This rejuvenation by purge receives high marks from Rikkyo University business professor Kazuo Noda[54] and from Eleanor M. Hadley, former Japan anti-trust specialist for the occupation forces,[55] who see it as having promoted a generational change in top corporate echelons, thereby lowering executives' average age by almost ten years and providing more active management. Irrespective of how one views rejuvenation, the dissolution of the *zaibatsu* and the economic purge saw management of the old *zaibatsu* companies pass completely from the *zaibatsu* families to professional managers. As touched on earlier, the power of professional managers in Japan was considerable from a very early point and grew steadily throughout the Showa period. GHQ's extremely tough anti-monopoly/anti-capitalist policies, however, firmly established professional management power, which eventually was to act as a sturdy foundation for large Japanese corporations. Whereas capitalists in the old *zaibatsu* were effectively eliminated, professional managers in some instances started to become capitalists in peripheral companies.[56]

It would be mistaken, however, to view this development as simply having handed control to a group of new capitalist families. Instead, although the professional managers exhibited some of the traits of their predecessors, they

---

[53]*Ibid.*

[54]Kazuo Noda, *Sengo Nihon no Keieisha, Sengo Nihon no Keizai Seicho,* Ryutaro Komiya, ed., 1963.

[55]Eleanor M. Hadley, *Antitrust in Japan* (Princeton, 1970).

[56]Hankyu's Ichizo Kobayashi, Tokyu's Keita Goto, Seibu's Yasujiro Tsutsumi, Komatsu's Yoshinari Kawaai, and so on.

generally trained their successors in their own distinct image. Nevertheless, compared to the majority of big corporations, where there are no elements of capitalist-ownership, company and family businesses like Matsushita, Honda, Ohbayashi, Takeda, and Torii (all of which quickly took off after the war) were endowed with a highly capitalist type of vitality and were not very "bureaucratic" in nature.

One point that must be borne in mind concerning this process of *zaibatsu* dissolution and purge is that the economic bureaucracy--the Ministries of Finance, Commerce and Industry, and Agriculture and Forestry, etc.--was preserved virtually intact from the pre-war days. Moreover, financial institutions were exempted from decentralizing laws and were not broken up. As the author and Yukio Noguchi, an economist at Hitotsubashi University, wrote in a 1977 journal article, although no stone was left unturned in breaking up the military and the Ministry of Home Affairs (MHA), the economic bureaucracy centering around the Ministry of Finance was successful in keeping virtually its entire pre-war structure, although it did undergo partial changes with the introduction of the National Personnel Authority and amendments to the Government Officials Act. As an aside, the current structure of the MOF remains virtually unchanged from that of 1937, apart from the addition of the Securities Bureau (transferred from the Ministry of Commerce and Industry in 1941) and the Customs Bureau, as well as a few nominal changes--e.g. the Foregn Exchange Bureau becoming the International Finance Bureau. Of the total 210,000 who were purged, only 2,000 bureaucrats outside the military were affected. The great majority came from the MHA; only nine were from the MOF.[57]

In other words, the basic structure of the public sector that was formed between the late 1920s and early 1930s was in fact strengthened at this time. Although professional managers in the private sector were filling the vacuum left behind by the *zaibatsu* break-up, the economic bureaucracy was consolidating both its pre- and post-war public sector foundations, and putting the finishing touches on its framework for "mutual understanding" with the private sector. From the war's immediate aftermath until the 1950s, the public sector was exceptionally strong due to the need to rebuild an economy that effectively was in ruins. War-time control of economic management also remained to a large extent. Yet this control gradually started to evolve into the mixed Japanese economy that was outlined in the previous section, as the trend towards deregulation and internationalization grew, especially in trade and foreign exchange.

---

[57]Eisuke Sakakibara and Yukio Noguchi, "Okurasho/Nichigin Ocho no Bunseki-Soryokusen Keizai Taisei no Shuen," *Chuo Koron,* August, 1977.

It has already been mentioned that Japan's regime of indirect finance, of which public finance is an important part, played a significant role in the rebuilding and maturation of the economy. The fact that financial institutions, like the economic bureaucracy, were preserved intact during the process of *zaibatsu* dissolution and purges is instrumental here.

GHQ's first round of tough economic reform, which started with the break up of the *zaibatsu* and progressed to agricultural land reform and purges, created a strong backlash not only in Japan but in the United States as well, especially in financial circles. The January 27, 1947, issue of *Newsweek*, for example, reported that 25,000 to 30,000 entrepreneurs considered to be "the brains of Japan" had been purged "unexpectedly" by "America, that bastion of capitalism," and were of two minds as to "whether they should become black-market racketeers or communists."[58] As the Cold War escalated, this backlash within the United States gradually led to modifications of the early course of GHQ reform.

Against the backdrop of a developing Cold War structure centered on events in China, Kenneth C. Royall, Secretary of the Army, stressed in January, 1948 the importance of "Japanese economic autonomy," claiming that "we maintain as our resolute goal the establishment of a strong and stable Japan capable of full independence, a self-sufficient and democratic Japan which can act as a buffer against the threat of a new, all-out warfare which may take place in the Far East." Subsequently, Undersecretary of the Army William Draper visited Japan with a mission led by Chemical Bank Chairman Percy Hampton Johnson, who produced a report on the basic course of Japanese occupation policy. This report led to a string of policy changes--redemption sums being scaled down and decentralization laws being relaxed--and ultimately led to the Dodge Plan, which formed the basis of the post-war economic policy regime.[59]

A critically important point for the later establishment of indirect financing methods was the fact that the break up of the Big Five banks was cancelled and the proposed comprehensive financial reform known as the Kagle Proposal was never put into practice. With regard to the break-up of the Big Five, the progressive Edward C. Welsh, director of the occupation's Antitrust/Cartel Division, was fiercely opposed by the chief of the Economic Sciences Bureau chief, William F. Marquat, and in the end joined the list of other occupation New Dealers (deputy chief of the government section, Charles L. Kades, labor division chief, Theodore

---

[58]Quoted in "Showa Zaiseishi-Shusen kara Kowa made," (Vol.13, *Toyo Keizai Shinposha,* 1976), p. 301. Various facts quoted in the main text are largely based on the exacting research carried out by Ikuhiko Hata in this work.

[59]Eisuke Sakakibara and Yukio Noguchi, op. cit.

Cohen and his successor, James S. Killen, and government section chief, Alfred R. Hussey) who had left the supreme allied command by 1950.

Although the New Dealers and their early reforms made their mark in the form of agricultural land reform and the dissolution of the *zaibatsu*, their departure saw the economic policy regime take a more classical turn, as evident from the introduction of the Dodge Plan, named after occupation financial advisor Joseph M. Dodge. As is well known, the December, 1948, blueprint for deflation consisted of balanced budgets, better tax collection, an end to *Fukkin* loans (government loans made through the Reconstruction and Development Corporation), and a fixed, single-tier exchange rate of ¥360 to the dollar. In other words, the plan was an orthodox prescription in a classical framework. Alongside the tax system set up by advisor Carl S. Shoup, the Dodge Plan formed the basis of economic policy in Japan during its high growth period.

Nevertheless, a series of easy money measures was implemented in order to alleviate some of the deflationary shock caused by the Plan. One example was large-volume lending with funds derived both from Bank of Japan loans and U.S. aid funds supplied by the Special Account for Industrial Investment. This method of fund supply later became systematized, with the financial institutions that were exempted from dissolution gradually establishing themselves as the leaders of the corporate groupings.

Yoshio Suzuki, President of the Nomura Research Institute, argues that this entrenched, post-war financial system was typified by over-lending, over-borrowing, uneven fund distribution, and the dominance of indirect financing. It was supported by a policy of artificially low interest rates, the non-internationalization of finance, and an export/investment-led economic structure.[60]

At the same time, it must be noted that this financial system, which was based on indirect finance, was part of the "Japanese mixed economic system" that was gradually formed throughout the Showa period, rather than the result of Japan being a backward country. In other words, during Taisho and early Showa--the period Nakamura refers to as the classical capitalist era--direct financial markets were flourishing in Japan, and were centered around the bond market.[61] The amount of corporate issues grew from an average of ¥20 million in 1912-14 to more than ¥100 million by 1919, and climbed even further by 1928, to ¥1.2 billion. Elsewhere, the short-term money markets developed substantially after World War

---

[60]Yoshio Suzuki, *Gendai Nihon Kinyuron* (Toyo Keizai Shinposha, September, 1974).

[61]Nakamura, *Showa Keizaishi, op. cit.*

I, and the call market was entering its phase of greatest maturity in 1926 with a jump in bill-broker stock banks and increasingly mature funding capacity.

A prominent feature of this period was the extremely high proportion of direct finance in the supply of industrial funds, corresponding to a direct/indirect ratio (change in industrial funds) of 86:14 on a flow basis in 1931. After the Great Depression, the ensuing reorganization of banks, and the enactment of the Fund Adjustment Act, this ratio fell gradually from 70:30 in 1935 to 50:50 in 1940. It finally rebounded in 1945 to stand at 10:90.[62] Due to the establishment of balanced budgets and low interest policy as the Japanese norm, which can be traced to the Dodge Plan, this 1945 ratio was maintained for 30 years after the war.

Moreover, since a large portion of pre-war direct finance took the shape of stock ownership by holding companies within the *zaibatsu*, or the provision of credit by *zaibatsu* companies, the break-up of the *zaibatsu* destroyed this *zaibatsu*-centered system of credit. It was therefore impossible to recreate the basic pattern of Taisho-early Showa direct finance. That is to say, it was only when the dissolution of the *zaibatsu* coincided with the preservation of the financial institutions that a regime centered on indirect finance could become the norm.

A graphic illustration of the continuity between pre-war and post-war financial systems is probably the Industrial Bank of Japan. As stated earlier, the IBJ rapidly increased its amount of funds around 1935 and developed into an important backer for the so-called new industrial concerns. After the war, too, it and two other banks--which also were long-term credit banks--were granted an issuing monopoly on financial debentures by the Law Concerning Bond Issues by Banks. As a result, the IBJ was placed in an extremely strategic position for the process of high economic growth. Thus along with the Japan Development Bank, the Export-Import Bank of Japan, and the old *zaibatsu*-affiliated city banks, the IBJ and the other two long-term credit banks acted as a major pipeline for supplying funds to industry.

Moreover, the IBJ's semi-public nature meant that it often became lead manager or played a leading role in funding syndicates. It also came to wield substantial influence not only in the indirect finance market but in the direct finance market as well, in its capacity as a member of the *Kisaikai* (a bond issue syndicate with the major city banks) and as a key member of the government bond and

---

[62]For more details on this see Yuichiro Nagatomi's, "Antei Seichoka no Kinyu Kozo," *Finance,* February, 1977.

government-guaranteed bond underwriting syndicate. Former president Isao Masamune has made the following comments on the role of the IBJ.

It is very different from the pre-war days of the special banks, but more emphasis is now placed on a supporting role, with more joint financing. We have reached an age of technological innovation and large-scale investment that makes it difficult to carry everything out within the affiliated group, and there are many cases when the participation of the neutral IBJ makes things go smoother.

When trying to follow a policy of fostering corporate issues in an undeveloped capital market, a lot of the parties involved experience a conflict of opinions concerning the size of the issue, the terms and conditions, the rating, the best timing, and so on. They often need a suitable moderator to help them decide in the limited time available. The IBJ has traditionally been involved in this area from pre-war days and at times will promote itself in this role. On the other hand, it is becoming increasingly common to be asked to act as the commissioned bank and issue coordinator.[63]

Blossoming into a High Growth Economy

The Japanese economy is undergoing an historical period of ascendancy. And it is the unleashing of the nation's creative abilities that is the driving force behind this historical leap. The fact that economic growth reached 17 percent in 1959, and that the economy is extremely stable despite this sharp expansion, is proof of the resilience of the Japanese economy. The desire and ability of private sector entrepreneurs, managers, technicians, and workers to rationalize, modernize and improve productivity is already evident from this performance. The Japanese economy should continue to grow at this fast pace if we do not neglect to further foster and consolidate these strengths. I believe we are capable of not just doubling the GNP, but of almost tripling it. This sort of high growth will undoubtedly revolutionize the entire span of economic activity.[64]

Between April and June of 1960, both the Diet and Japan itself were rocked by a series of violent demonstrations over the U.S.-Japan Security Treaty. It fell upon a new cabinet led by Hayato Ikeda to take over from the government of Nobusuke

---

[63]Kichi Shimura, *Sengo Sangyoshi e no Shogen 5-Kigyo Shudan no Keisei* (Mainichi Shimbunsha, 1979).

[64]Osamu Shimomura, "Seicho Seisaku no Kihon Mondai," *Kinyu Zaisei Jijo*, No. 518, July 11, 1960.

Kishi, which resigned from office after the renewal of the security treaty. The new Prime Minister proclaimed from on high his "plan to double income" and successfully switched from the "season of politics" to the "season of economics." The brain behind this "plan to double income" was the then Executive Director of the Japan Development Bank and former-MOF officer, Osamu Shimomura. Shimomura had already put forward in the 1950s his so-called "Shimomura theory," which was Keynesian in nature and based in particular on the Keynesian theories of income determination and multiplication. This in turn formed the basis of Ikeda's economic policy, mediated especially by his policy advisor, Toshio Tamura of Ikeda's LDP faction, the Kochikai.

As is well known, the "plan to double income" aimed at achieving its goal over a ten-year period, and therefore required annual average growth of 7.2 percent. Yet because the government added the goal of achieving 9 percent growth in the plan's first three years, its average growth rate objective became 7.8 percent. As Shimomura himself acknowledged, however, annual growth rates in the last half of the 1950s had already reached 7-8 percent. Thus the "plan to double income" could well be seen as an attempt merely to maintain this pace over the next ten years. He argued:

> It is damaging to underestimate unnecessarily the growth capacity of the Japanese economy. Nor is it realistic always to presuppose a worst-case scenario in either a domestic or international context. What we should be looking at is determining just what can be achieved in the next ten years through the stimulation of national creative abilities under as realistic a scenario as possible.[65]

The 9 percent and 7.2 percent targets--or what to Shimomura was "realistic," and in fact low when viewed in hindsight--were seen at the time as being extremely optimistic. A great many "pessimistic" theorists believed annual growth of more than 3-4 percent to be impossible, and predicted inflation and balance of payments crises when growth in fact exceeded this figure. Shimomura was more or less in the minority. Yet in 1956--three years before the income-doubling plan--during the "growth/cycle or inventory debate" that he engaged with Yonosuke Goto of the Economic Planning Agency Research Bureau, Shimomura had already shown that plant and equipment investment basically constituted investment for modernization and rationalization, and therefore was a factor in raising supply capacity. He had further argued in 1957 that there was no need to fear inflation, thereby indicating

---

[65]*Ibid.*

the sophistication of his theory of long-term growth induced by plant-and-equipment investment.[66]

The Japanese economy subsequently continued to grow in an extremely stable pattern of "investment generating investment," with real GNP rising at an average of 11.6 percent in the years 1960-69--almost 4 percent higher than the targeted figure of 7.8 percent. To quote Shimomura, "The Japanese economy was an even greater optimist than I was."[67] As a result, Japanese GNP reached ¥3.5 trillion, which even in real terms corresponded to 1.56 times the targeted amount. Annual growth in per capita income also far outstripped its original goal of 6.9 percent and reached 10.4 percent, thereby enabling Japan to gradually join the club of "wealthy nations."

The causes of Japan's high growth have been analyzed a great many times, and although there is no need here for a comprehensive review, several points relevant to our structural analysis of the Japanese economy need to be noted.

The first is that the groundwork had been laid by the break-up of the *zaibatsu* and the purging of capitalists from the corporate side (especially the large corporations--i.e., the instigators of the growth-producing plant and equipment investment) for pursuing a decisive strategy of "segregation of ownership and management." The way also was clear for young, professional managers to pursue new goals enthusiastically. As a result of the economic purge and the departure of a great many leaders and "head clerks" from their posts, members of the so-called upper-middle group (men in their mid-forties, section and division chiefs) found themselves in positions of authority where they could manage operations aggressively. Moreover, aggressive management was unavoidable given the fiercer competition brought on by the collapse of the old order, by the decentralization laws, and by the Anti-trust Law.

The so-called peoplism management approach put forward by Itami--based on employee sovereignty and centering mainly on the professional manager--was the basic structure that supported this corporate activity. Itami sees "peoplism management" competition as being characterized by the concepts of long-term, multi-dimensional and collective competition with clearly visible competitors, and

---

[66]Osamu Shimomura, Collected Papers, *Keizai Seicho no Jitsugen no tame ni* (Kohchi Kai, 1958) pp. 227-312.

[67]Osamu Shimomura, *Nihon Keizai Seichorono*, (Kinyu Zaisei Jijo Kenkyuukai, 1962).

compares it to "capitalist" short-term, one-dimensional, individual, and faceless competition.[68]

Additionally, in a setting of high savings rates and generous credit expansion by the government and the Bank of Japan, the financial sector and banks in particular responded positively to corporate fund demand. The financial sector's ability to do so without triggering inflation stemmed from an extraordinarily high national desire to save (as Japanese society became increasingly middle-class), as well as from the aforementioned fierce competition over savings that took place in the financial and the postal savings system and agricultural cooperatives. Incidentally, the GNP ratio of Japanese financial institutions' liabilities around 1955, or at the start of the high growth period, was rising sharply.[69] Japanese financial institutions were able to answer the burgeoning demands for funds during the high growth period by quickly increasing deposits and financial debentures. Certainly BOJ lending also increased, yet the greater share of increased liabilities corresponded to increased savings by the general populace.

The high Japanese savings rate has been analyzed as basically falling within the framework of the life-cycle hypothesis, with various explanations being put forward--including the impacts of the bonus system, of the high costs of education and housing, and of retirement pensions. Let us note here, however, that the post-war Japanese social structure of high social mobility combined with an equitable distribution of income to provide an extremely advantageous environment for such high savings.

Another important factor behind high growth was a revolution in technology. It is often stressed that foreign technology was brought into Japan to fill the vacuum created by the war, but a large number of technologies had been developed in Japan both before and during the war, the great majority of which were military-related. The significant role played by this technological stockpile even as foreign technology was brought in should not be overlooked. The evolution of applied technology, which went together with the many technologies introduced from abroad to create Japan's unique system of low-cost mass production, was clearly the end result of a cumulative process that started before the war. Nakamura speaks as follows of the war-time legacy:

> Behind post-war heavy and chemical industrialization we find that not only had a large number of suitable plants and equipment been installed for

---

[68]Itami, *Jinpon Shugi Kigyo, op. cit.*

[69]See Sakakibara, Feldman, and Harada, *The Japanese Financial System in Comparative Perspective, op. cit.*.

the war-time military industries, but that trained technicians and workers had also learned their trades in these factories. Just as war-time machine gun factories turned out sewing machines and optical weapons factories made cameras or binoculars, the reserve of plants, equipment, and technology, as well as the labor force, had a very significant impact on the future direction of the Japanese economy. The subcontractor system that became so widely used after the war actually had its beginnings during the war. Large corporations involved in military production at first followed the principle of in-house production for all parts, but gradually began to subcontract out to smaller companies. Although this was an emergency measure to raise production, at the same time it was also an opportunity to improve technology at smaller companies and raise production levels. It was also a chance to make the union of large and smaller companies conclusive. It was of decisive significance that the smaller companies in the heavy and chemical industries developed on the basis of stable and secure orders, and it is here that the source of relations between smaller companies and parent companies should be sought.[70]

Debate concerning the role of the government in the process of high growth has persisted and even in recent times revolves around the central concept of "industrial policy." Since Norman Macrae first published a long two-part article titled "Consider Japan" in *The Economist* in September, 1962, which sang the praises of high growth, non-Japanese analysts in particular have put forward many different arguments and stressed the government's role.[71] The so-called "Japan Incorporated theory" is typical of this sort of analysis. Chalmers Johnson, to cite one prominent example, highlights the government's role, and that of MITI in particular, to an excessive degree.[72] Subsequent analyses of Japan's politics or economy by Japanologists have rejected such extreme arguments, confining themselves to something more eclectic, such as the aforementioned Samuels' framework of "mutual understanding."

Of course, the tide of war-time control never completely abated, and various direct or indirect government regulations and instances of administrative guidance were of great import especially from the 1950s to the 1960s. Rather than being the result of a specific plan, however, it was because of the very structure of the "Japanese mixed economy" itself that the public and private

---

[70]Nakamura, *Nihon Keizai-Sono Seicho to Kozo, op cit.*

[71]See *The Economist*, September 1, 1962, pp. 787-823 and September 8, 1962, pp. 907-936

[72]Johnson, *MITI and the Japanese Miracle, op. cit.*

competitive/cooperative system functioned smoothly. It is well known that the public sector--revolving as it did around public works, furbished social infrastructure in the form of roads, ports, the bullet train, and so on--created a substantial external economic effect for the private sector. It is also understood that the public sector supported growth from the sidelines by channelling postal and pension funds though the Fiscal Investment and Loan Plan to the Japanese Development Bank, The Export-Import Bank of Japan, and the Electric Power Development Company. Plainly, the Ministries of International Trade and Industry, Construction, Transport, Agriculture and Fisheries, as well as Finance, also played a considerable role.

Yet the most accurate interpretation is that rather than the government trying to implement this approach in line with some kind of comprehensive growth policy or industrial policy, the public sector--which had gradually established several entrepreneurial arms during the Showa period and World War II--acted with and in response to the private sector in developing various areas of operations. Undeniably, these operations were more or less controlled either in terms of expenditure, taxes, or loans. But as pointed out earlier, the planners or instigators came at the end of the line. To say therefore that because they had control of the budget, these operations were implemented as part of a centrally coordinated plan is a mistake. The basic pattern of the dissemination of information and operational responsibilities, as well as the centralization of personnel and budget, exists both within the private as well as within the public sector, albeit to a differing degree.

Although it has given rise to considerable misinterpretation and confusion, the Japanologists' analyses have made one valuable contribution to greater understanding--they were largely responsible for overturning at a grass-roots level the "backward syndrome" that existed in Japanese academic circles as well as in Japanese society at large. To cite an example, thanks to the work of James C. Abeggglen--long-time Tokyo Representative of the Boston Consulting Group--and others, the seniority system, life-time employment, and company trade unions, once interpreted as typical illustrations of Japanese backwardness, have now come to be thought of as advantages.[73] Subsequent analyses by Western Japanologists or Japanese researchers have criticized "cultural arguments" along the lines made by Abbegglen, and have approached the matter with a more rational model.[74] Yet the high-economic-growth and Macrae/Abbegglen-style writings had such a tremendous impact that nowadays it is the arrogance of Japanese managers regarding "Japanese management" that receives considerable emphasis. Still it is

---

[73]James C. Abbegglen, *The Japanese Factory* (Free Press, 1985).

[74]M. Aoki, ed., *The Economic Analysis of the Japanese Firm* (North Holland, 1984).

only natural that the inferiority complex felt by the Japanese vis-a-vis the West since Meiji has been somewhat rectified by high economic growth. With the exception of a few such as Osamu Shimomura, however, the fact that only Western journalists and critics were capable of stimulating this reappraisal does raise serious doubts as to the nature of the Japanese intellectual community since Meiji times.[75]

---

[75]See the Supplement for more details on this point.

V. Internationalization: A Growing Dilemma for the Japanese Mixed Economy

Borderless Economies and the "Closed" Japanese Economy

While the Japanese socio-economy was gradually forming the framework for a mixed economy during the Showa Period, the rest of the world was also undergoing a metamorphosis after the Great Depression. Classical capitalism steadily yielded to a mixed economy.

From the late 1920s to the early 1930s, one industrialized country after another left the gold standard for a floating exchange-rate regime, with protectionist tendencies gaining ground all the while. In time, the framework for a mixed economy gradually fell into place, and state intervention in international finance and trade advanced on the domestic front through the establishment of a central bank system and the expansion of its powers, as well as through greater participation by the fiscal authorities in overall demand policy.

Obvious instances of the former in the United States include the establishment of the Federal Deposit Insurance Corporation (1933) and the enactment of the Glass-Steagall Act (also 1933). John Maynard Keynes' *General Theory* (1936) and Franklin Roosevelt's New Deal are both well known examples of the latter. Although the Second World War had a substantial impact on the global economic system, it did not change the overall system as much as is often believed. Rather, it is probably more accurate to view the Second World War as having put the finishing touches on the regime of U.S. international economic leadership that began to evolve around 1930.

It is true that there was a great deal of soul-searching as the General Agreement on Tariffs and Trade (GATT) and Bretton Woods systems were established to replace the excessively protectionist and exploitive policies of the 1930s and 1940s. Yet both the central bank-based system of monetary policy and international controls on short-term capital-as-money were maintained. Theoretical frameworks for each country's overall demand policies were also consolidated and orderly tracks laid down.

From the late 1940s to the 1950s, J.R. Hicks and Paul Samuelson systematized the new school of so-called Keynesian economics and consolidated the theoretical foundations for "neo-classical" macroeconomics and enabled text books to speak of "the mixed economy system". Certain scholars regard this development as the vulgarization or Americanization of Keynesian economics. It is true that "neo-classical" theory played its own part in the establishment of a regime centered on the United States. Nevertheless, it is probably best to view this response of the economics field in the context of the broad global move towards a mixed economy system dating from the 1930s.

True, the GATT/Bretton Woods regime differed essentially from the "system" of the 1930s and 1940s in that it aimed at free trade and the free movement of capital (more precisely, long-term capital), and established a fixed exchange-rate regime based on the gold/dollar standard. All the same, the stress on continuity within countries between the pre- and post-war eras is justified because the excessive attention paid to the international front, with its establishment of multilateral institutions and the setting of "liberalization" goals, tended to lead to neglect of the uninterrupted nature of domestic economic regimes. Although the issue of continuity and rupture is, of course, relative, it is still most useful to view the period from 1930 to the 1970s as a single phase when looking at various economies around the world from the standpoint of a "mixed economy system".

The characteristics of the 1930s-1970s period become clear when they are compared to the 1980s, especially from the perspective of domestic and international finance. During the earlier period, domestic finance was tightly regulated, with international movements of capital being relatively limited apart from those of an official nature. For example, syndicated loans to developing countries by Japanese, U.S., and European banks began to rise sharply in the 1970s, essentially creating the third world debt crisis. Yet there were virtually no *private* international financial transactions with developing countries from the time of the Great Depression until the mid-seventies. It is well known of course that extremely large volumes of capital moved from Europe to Latin America from the mid-1800s until the 1920s, and that these helped trigger the global depression. If the period up to 1930 is viewed as one of laissez-faire or financial capital, the period 1930-1970 could well be viewed as one of state economic intervention and financial control.

It is during the 1970s that cracks started to emerge in the "mixed economy system" based on this kind of financial control and the regulation of short-term capital transactions. Due to rampant inflation and defeat in Vietnam, liberalism in the United States reached its lowest ebb since the 1930s. A new conservatism and a neo-classical tide were on the rise. The August 15, 1971 suspension of gold and dollar convertability, or the so-called Nixon Shock, ultimately led to the introduction of a floating exchange-rate regime in February-March 1973.

Elsewhere, the rapid expansion of the Eurodollar market in the late 1960s had an enormous impact on financial markets around the world after the oil shocks of 1973-74, and financial deregulation in the United States and the sharp jump in world private financial transactions both gathered speed. Offshore markets like London, Luxembourg, Hong Kong, Singapore, and even the Bahamas and the Cayman Islands became centers for free international financial transactions, recycling so-called oil money and, in the 1980s, rechanneling the funds of balance of payments surplus countries like Japan and West Germany.

The "Euromarket's" unregulated financial transactions no longer confined themselves to the Euromarket, but gradually began to affect first New York, then London and Tokyo, accelerating the pace of deregulation in those markets.[76] Just as the United States underwent rapid deregulation due to the sharp expansion of the Eurodollar market, so too has Japan followed a faster path of financial deregulation after the Yen-Dollar Commission Report of 1984 on deregulation and after the expansion in Euroyen and other transactions in London and New York.

Although it still suffers some imperfections, it is in this context that the "world financial market" has gradually taken shape, with money markets and foreign exchange markets around the globe firmly fused together. Even when interest rate movements in one country are not tightly enough linked to other markets because of various partial barriers, for example, inevitably some profitable form of innovation that circumvents the problem is quickly developed. As a result, it is becoming increasingly rare for financiers in the major economies to make policy decisions on either fund appropriations or investments within a purely domestic framework. Key currencies and their financial commodities are now traded 24 hours around the globe at basically the same price.

---

[76]See Eisuke Sakakibara's "Kokusai Kinyu Shijo no Hatten to Sono Eikyo," Ryuichiro Tachi, and Shoichi Rohyama, eds. *Nihon no Kinyu: II Kokusaika no Tenbo* (Tokyo University Press, June, 1987) for a detailed analysis on this point.

The establishment of a "global financial market" in the 1980s and the accompanying radical internationalization of economic activity has eroded the concept of national borders in economic activity. The world is very much poised on the threshold of "borderless economies." Nakatani points out the need to acknowledge the "historical fact that 'systemic internationalization' has begun in earnest" as a result of the increasingly borderless nature of economic activity. In other words:

> In almost all cases, the establishment of a "system" to date only required that domestic conditions be taken into consideration. Within the framework of national sovereignty, the choice of "system" was determined by the wishes of the people according to democratic rules. With economic activity becoming internationalized to this degree and the true significance of national borders eroded, it is impossible to ignore the impact of international movements of economic resources on the systemic decision-making process. Even if policy officials try to emphasize domestic interests and maintain a domestic-oriented system, that system will be untenable in the long run as long as it is out of kilter with those of other countries, because as long as a "more profitable system" for economic entities exists elsewhere, those entities will exit, leaving a "hollowed-out" economy in their wake.[77]

The issue of systemic internationalization accompanying increasingly borderless economies does not pertain to Japan alone. It is more a question of how the mixed economy system that started in the 1930s will evolve in the future. What is especially important for Japan is the fact that the current regime--our "Japanese model of a mixed economy"--has some sharply pronounced features compared to other major economies.

Specifically, the Japanese system is characterized by the internalization of the market and the guarantee of broad-ranging rights for participants. As such it is more closed or club-like in nature than the U.S. or European systems. For the participants, it is extremely egalitarian and stable, but for outsiders, it appears both opaque and unfair. Indeed, in many cases the barriers are high for entry into Japanese organizations, and this problem is especially serious for non-Japanese, who do not share a common Japanese cultural denominator. These characteristics of the Japanese mixed economy largely explain the never-ending stream of criticism about "closedness" even in areas where fair treatment is guaranteed either legally or systemically.

---

[77]I. Nakatani, "Borderless Economies," in *Sakoku Kokka Nippon e no Keisho* (Nihon Keizai Shimbunsha, July 10, 1987).

Nakatani has argued that it is the co-existence of "easily internationalized areas" and "not easily internationalized areas" that is a major cause of "international friction," and it would seem that even in the large corporate sector-- considered to be a comparatively easy area to internationalize--the internationalization of its Japanese characteristics involves many difficulties.[78] Important in this sense is the point made by Ronald Dore of the University of London and MIT that although Japanese companies act universally and European companies are heading in the same direction, he would not wish to work for a Japanese company.[79] In other words, although the large Japanese corporate organization is both rational and efficient, and meets certain humanitarian demands, it is unsatisfying in terms of Western ways of thinking or general liberalism. The big question for Japanese companies in the future will be how to fill this gap.

Elsewhere, the public sector--especially construction and agriculture--is one of Nakatani's "difficult to internationalize areas," and is highly likely to become the focus of "international friction" in the future. Systemic and structural reform in this sector, with its complex web of regional society, cooperative organizations, bureaucratic mechanisms, and politics, is no easy task, however, as will be shown later. The situation differs completely from that of the large corporate sector, which is forcibly confronted by competition in the market.

Reform of this public sector represents a great turning point in the structure of Japanese society, and it is not as easy as liberal-minded intellectuals insist. The "Japanese model of a mixed economy" was established during Showa on a course determined by previous historical developments. The changes it undergoes in the future will depend entirely upon how the public sector responds to the tide of internationalization.

Maturation and Stagnation in the Public Sector: Politicization of the Bureaucracy and Bureaucratization of the Party

With internationalization and deregulation forging rapidly ahead, the pace of change in economic transactions--especially financial transactions--has not just increased, but undergone an acute acceleration. The advent of 24-hour trading in a global market has set the economic clock whizzing.

---

[78]Nakatani, "Borderless Economies," *op. cit.*

[79]R. Dore, *Igirisu no Kojo: Nihon no Kojo*, translated by K. Yamanouchi and K. Nagayasu (Chikuma Shobo, October, 1987).

At the same time, with its complicated system centering on the traditional nation-state, the political clock does not seem able to keep up with the economic clock. Many of the problems that plague the major economies of the world, Japan's included, stem from the significant lag between the two.

Generally speaking, in politically and administratively mature countries, the higher the degree of democracy, the greater the decentralization of power, the broader the base of participation, and the more complex the accompanying processes. This tendency is especially pronounced in Japan, where decentralization of power and broad participation are extremely well developed.

As mentioned earlier, Japanese organization, both in the large corporate and public sectors, is characterized by a marked decentralization of information and business authority. In the large firm, however, authority over staff appointments and budget decisions is centralized, enabling the firm to make strategic responses to new developments. In the public sector, by contrast, authority over nearly everything--appointments and budget matters, over information and business operations alike--is considerably diffuse. Thus, strategic decision making is extremely difficult. Authority over appointments in the public sector, both pre- and post-war, has been characterized by a vertical compartmentalization along ministry lines. This pattern has been cited as one of the major causes behind the military's-- and particularly the army's--domination of Japanese politics in the run-up to World War II. Even after the war, as the activities supervised by each ministry have come to overlap, a ministerial sense of propriety in the personnel area has often thwarted decision making of a strategic nature.

However, compared to a large firm with 50-150,000 employees at most, centralizing authority over the 490,000 employees in the central government alone is no easy task. One of the underlying ideas behind both the Temporary Commission for Administrative Reform and greater utilization of the private sector is to organize the public sector more along the lines of large Japanese firms. Yet this notion inevitably begs the question of centralizing authority over staff appointments. Is such a development possible? More to the point, is it even desirable?

The author's answer to both questions is an unequivocal "no." First, the public sector is too large for authority over personnel appointments to be centralized. Moreover, the shape of Japanese politics and administration, as well as their mutual relationship, are different from America's, for instance, where the president makes most appointments. As is well known, the Japanese Prime Minister's term of office runs from two to four years, each cabinet usually averaging one year, and appointees are almost always duly elected, professional politicians. As was also mentioned earlier, politicians, backed up mainly by the party and the Diet, wield considerable power and influence over policy, but do not necessarily play leading roles as heads of the administrative branch of government. If in such a setting powers of appointment were centralized in the Prime Minister's Office, for example, personnel decisions would become considerably more politicized even than at present. The subordination of the administrative branch to the legislative branch of government would be reinforced and the neutrality and continuity of both the judiciary and administration would be compromised.

In a case like that of the United States, where the head of the executive branch--the president--is elected separately from the members of the legislative branch, and cabinet members are mainly chosen from experts from the private sector, it may be possible even with a wide range of political appointments to maintain the executive branch's neutrality from politics. Under the Japanese system, however, it would be extremely difficult to switch to the American model at the present juncture. Even the system in Britain, another parliamentary democracy, contrasts strikingly with Japan's. In Britain, the independence of the bureaucracy from politics is maintained by cabinet appointees who are more often than not specialists in their fields rather than politicians. Once again, in Britain's case, the parties themselves are strong and can send experts into Parliament by arranging for them to run for seats in so-called safe districts, thereby avoiding the rigors of electioneering. This feature only highlights further the idiosyncratic nature of the "election-centered" Japanese system, where cabinet seats are parcelled out according to the number of times politicians have been elected. Of course, one should not deny the importance of "elections" in a democratic system, but selecting cabinet officials according to the number of successful elections and not according to ability can only be called a peculiar product of post-war Japanese politics.

There is a very strong likelihood that, under this very different Japanese system, the centralization of authority over personnel appointments via the Prime Minister's Office would give new powers of control to the party, further subordinate the administrative branch of government to the individual interests that influence elections, and also threaten the neutrality of the administrative branch. It is by no means desirable that personnel appointments in the administration become more politicized that at present, when the original democratic pattern of establishing a grand political and administrative framework as well as a policy regime by election, and when implementing that policy by a professional and neutral administration both have changed considerably under the Japanese post-war regime.

That "the politicization of the bureaucracy and the bureaucratization of politics" is often raised even in present circumstances seems to stem from the fact that appointments in the administrative branch can be swayed by the party's *zoku* representatives or factional considerations. Needless to say, the role of the legislative branch and the political parties that are intrinsic to it is to establish a large policy framework by newly enacting or altering the laws comprising the nation's basic systemic framework, and not to implement individual policies. Nevertheless, since pre-war times, Japan's political parties and its parliamentary politicians have had the function of checking policy implementation by the bureaucracy. This role, as well as developments in the post-war election system, has led to the close ties with regional public works and other activities. As has already been described, regional bodies (such as municipal government and cooperatives, etc.) have come to play the role of business instigators, and they expect the central bureaucracy to finance such business. This is where the role of the politician takes on a hue more entrepreneurial than that of the legislator. This is where the political parties, encumbered with so many individual entrepreneurs, as well as the political system itself, take on the flavor of a business association covering two major areas--namely elections and public works.

We have argued that the Japanese economy is a two-dimensional structure consisting of a large corporate sector and the public sector. Within this two-dimensional structure, the Keidanren and other major business associations form the top political structure for the large corporate sector. The ruling party forms the top structure for the public sector's business activities. It is only natural that the ruling party performs this function, and that the support organizations of individual politicians should establish the public sector's business system and work to cement it.

Elsewhere, as the party structure--including the Policy Coordination Committee and various policy committees--has evolved, the traditional bureaucratic structure has gradually strengthened its relations of interdependence with the party and the Diet. In addition, this bureaucratic structure has come to play a part of what should be the party's political function (not the high politics of foreign or military or macroeconomic policy, but the low politics of elections and public-sector works). There is some incompatibility between the neutrality that the bureaucracy should maintain as a policy implementing body and the functions involved in low politics, but it must be acknowledged that, for better or worse, the involvement of the Japanese bureaucracy in low politics is proceeding at a considerably accelerated pace.

Both in the pre- and post-war periods, the high-politics function of Japanese politics and administration has been performed by a few elder statesmen or certain influential politicians and bureaucratic structures. Despite the problems involved in dispersing power over appointments by using vertical organizations, some coordinating mechanism has been maintained, at least to a certain extent, because the budget has been controlled more or less collectively by the Ministry of Finance and other ministries' networks. Although the process is long and difficult, the major policies of the public sector require the acceptance of each spending ministry, the MOF, and the LDP. It is in this sense that budget compilation can be said to occupy a central place in the current Japanese decision-making process. As stated earlier, budget compilation is a bottom-up exercise, but the role of the top echelon of the bureaucracy and the party is by no means small, for it has the power of veto. Establishing priorities on a top-down basis, however, is quite different and will only grow more so, especially as the party and Diet structures become increasingly rigid and their relations of mutual dependence with the administrative structure gradually become systematic.

Although this trend may just be the natural result of a maturing Japanese socio-economy and the systemization of public-sector works, the gap between the public sector and the large corporate sector is by no means small. One reason, but certainly not the only one, is the greater difficulty of centralizing authority over personnel appointments in the public sector. As Nakatani points out, another major cause is that the Japanese public sector, with its present system of elections, is an area that is "hard to internationalize." Whereas from very early on large firms have been directly confronted by international friction and forced by overseas competition to reform, the public sector has nurtured the political regime to maturity and expanded this participation within the confines of a more or less closed system. Broader participation and response to public opinion in a mass society has greatly advanced the democratization and popularization of Japanese politics and has seen the Japanese political system mature in its own way. Indeed, politics in Japan has achieved a high degree of stability in the post-war period even when compared to other politically mature countries.

As already mentioned, the Japanese political system in itself is by no means backward or distorted, yet the fact that this process of political stabilization and maturation took place in a closed system has opened up a wider gap with the large corporate sector--where internationalization and deregulation have made significant gains--than in other countries. It is precisely because the systemic maturity and rigidity of the Japanese political structure can only be shaken by elections that elections have become so important, and that personnel and other practices are so dominated by elections (for example, the selection of cabinet members according to the number of times elected).

Still it is essential to understand that the Japanese public sector or the political/administrative regime is more decentralized and egalitarian than its U.S. or European counterparts, and in a certain sense forms the nucleus of an extremely humanitarian economic regime. Itami's peoplism, or the regional social structure I refer to as the owner-farmer doctrine, form the ideology behind this regime. At least in my eyes, this humanitarian outlook seems more desirable than so-called capitalistic ideology. True, certain aspects of this system have emerged only because it has been established under closed conditions. But to change the system unconditionally into a capitalistic one in a tide of internationalization, deregulation, and privatization is not the answer. The original thrust of the Temporary Commission for Administrative Reform and Privatization is apt to focus too much on internationalization and profit for profit's sake, and to overlook the Japanese public sector's good points. Although public organizations such as *Seikyo* and *Nokyo* do have problems of their own, their function as counterweights to their private sector analogs is quite useful, as analyzed earlier. Needless to say, the privatization of all sectors and domination by large firms would not be desirable at all.

Of course, systemic reform is needed in the Japanese public sector. But it is because of my respect for the humanitarian principles of this sector that I believe that the answer is to improve its efficiency significantly. This is also why it must be made into the sort of sector that can internationalize and maintain anthropocentrism. Given the difficulties involved in systemic reform, however, success will remain uncertain unless reform of a penetrating and realistic nature is pursued. Machiavelli put it well:

> In any event, it must be grasped that to take the lead and introduce a new order whose success is uncertain and that is fraught with danger is the most difficult thing to achieve. This is because the prince who attempts this will make an enemy of every person who has benefitted from the previous order. And because those who try to use the new order will only do so in a half-hearted, reluctant way. The reason for their half-heartedness is fear of someone who can create law at a whim on the one hand, and the suspicion that every man has on the other. In other words, it is because no one trusts the new until they experience thereof.[80]

Although there seems to be a general recognition of the need for systemic reform in the public sector, and of the direction it should take, reform requires a true sense of strategic thinking whenever the great majority of the nation has at least some vested interest in the status quo. It is also true that there is precious little scope for a strategist-leader in this mold to emerge in today's political goldfish bowl. Novelist Nanami Shiono's lamentation that "it is a long time since we have had a man who could do the inglorious but maintain this own integrity"[81] and her citing of Winston Churchill as an example thereof is quite appropriate, and in a certain sense an apt reflection of the times in which we live.

---

[80]Machiavelli, *The Prince*, as translated in Japanese by Yasushi Ikeda, *Chuo Koron*, March, 1975.

[81]Nanami Shiono, "Otoko no Shozo" (*Bungei Shunju*, December, 1986).

Changes in Japanese Management

The high growth of the Japanese economy and the energetic pursuit of business by Japanese firms both at home and abroad have drawn worldwide attention, and "Japanese-style management" has become extremely popular in recent years as a symbol of success. Yet "Japanese-style management" should be considered not as a management technique, but as one facet of a system based on the Japanese model of mixed economy. As Abegglen and Stoke explain,

. . . Japan's economic growth can be largely explained without touching upon the subject of Japanese management. . . . This is not to say that Japanese management is ineffectual. It is merely one of a number of factors. Rather than explaining Japan's economic success by Japanese style management, it is much more tenable to explain that Japan's economic prosperity aided the success of the *kaisha* [the Japanese firm]. It is because of a favorable economic climate that the *kaisha* was able to successfully implement a strategy for headlong growth."[82]

The author here is not attempting to stress the role of the government. Rather, I would like to point out that the Japanese firm, which Itami refers to as a peoplist firm, has had a common "culture" that it shares with society as a whole. Within that "corporate culture," those managers who responded adroitly to the surrounding environment and were ahead of their time were highly successful. Moreover, the "corporate culture" fostered during the Showa period tailored itself to suit global economic trends and Japan's relative international position. The issue now is whether it is possible to maintain this "corporate culture" and social paradigm, or if they must change qualitatively as today's powerful trends of internationalization and growing socio-economic maturity bring about significant changes.

Itami takes a more optimistic tone regarding the first issue of internationalization.

. . . I believe that peoplism can fulfill two of the basic elements of internationalization [functional universality and the dilemma caused by different speeds in the movement of people, money, and all else that accompanies internationalization]. Speaking plainly, fulfilling the first element (functional universality) requires that "peoplism can cross borders". Fulfilling the second element has a rather more positive meaning.

---

[82]James C. Abegglen and George Stoke, Shuichiro Ueda, trans., *Kaisha* (Kodansha, June, 1986).

Namely, that peoplism can contribute to solving the intrinsic dilemma of internationalization and that "it is precisely because firms are peoplistic that they can cross borders."

In fact, capitalism, too, is fairly well prepared to meet these two elements of the basic concept of internationalization. History speaks for the first element of functional universality. For the second element--the dilemma of internationalization--capitalism is basically a corporate system of economic and money principles, and as long as it can give priority to economic logic over political logic, it holds true that "it is precisely because firms are capitalistic that they can cross borders." As shown by U.S. companies going multinational as they set up production plants around the globe in their search for low production costs, it is definitely true that they wanted and were able to cross borders because they were capitalistic enterprises. When as today, however, political logic can no longer be ignored, capitalism alone is not sufficient to solve the dilemma of internationalization. Symbolically speaking, political logic involves people. That is why capitalism is not enough. It places too much emphasis on economic logic. Peoplism, however, is the logic of a corporate system focussed from the very start on people, and as such, it is disposed to respond to political logic. It is in this sense that it is more easily asserted that rather than capitalist, "it is precisely because firms are peoplistic that they can cross borders."[83]

Itami is probably right in terms of logical possibilities, but the fact that the Japanese model of mixed economy or the peoplistic firm has developed a more internalized labor and capital market than a purer capitalistic system, and that is dominated by long-term contractual relations, implies conversely that it has more *closed* tendencies. Thus internationalizing the Japanese system will be no easy task. It is of special interest how the existing Japanese system changes in world financial markets, where the pace of deregulation has been extremely fast. It is extremely interesting that Japanese management and personnel practices are eroding in what might be called capitalism's front-line market. Foreign exchange and bond dealers no longer fit into the old salary frameworks and have been head-hunted in quick succession by non-Japanese securities houses.

It is not my intention to go into a specific analysis of the question here, but merely to draw attention to the underlying existence of a closed Japanese system that might be termed "humanist seclusion". Hirotaka Takeuchi, a professor of business administration at Hitotsubashi University, presents some important statistics:

---

[83]Itami, *Jinponshugi Kigyo, op. cit.*

Let us compare this situation in Japan with that of other countries. According to 1986 data issued by the Organization for Economic Cooperation and Development, Switzerland has the highest percentage of foreigners in its population, with 14.6 percent (1985), followed by Belgium, with 9 percent (1983); West Germany, with 7.2 percent (1985); France, with 6.8 percent (1982); and Sweden, with 4 percent (1985). The Japanese figure of 0.7 percent pales to insignificance beside these statistics. The percentage of foreign students in higher education institutions in Japan (0.8 percent) is likewise dwarfed by the corresponding figures of 12 percent in France, 7.9 percent in Britain, 5.9 percent in West Germany, and 4.7 percent in the United States.[84]

It is of course foolhardy to debate simply on the basis of comparisons with Europe and so on, where historical and cultural backgrounds differ so greatly. Yet it is true, as Takeuchi points out, that Japan's legal system--namely, the Immigration Control and Refugee Recognition Law and the Japanese Nationality Act--is more closed than Europe's or America's, and that the infrastructure for exchange students and trainees is sadly lacking. This reality, coupled with the closed mentality of the Japanese vis-a-vis things foreign, creates a major barrier to the internationalization of the labor force.[85]

Apart from the question of foreign workers, the closed nature of the Japanese system has been widely cited in the area of access to information. Successive leaks of insider information about stocks may also appear "unfair" to foreigners, and dissatisfaction is smoldering over the lack of national treatment in this area of information access in general.

Even if this "closedness" in the areas of personnel and information is not an inevitable accompaniment to the Japanese model of a mixed economy, or to Itami's peoplistic management theory, it is not completely unrelated either. This "closednesss," moreover, is quite capable of hindering attempts to internationalize the Japanese model.

---

[84]Hirotaka Takeuchi, "Immigration Reform for an Open Society," *Japan Echo* XIV, No. 4, 1987.

[85]". . . in the 'Survey on National Living Preferences' released by the Economic Planning Agency in September 1986 . . . fewer than 30 percent were in favor of long-term influx, such as increases in foreign employees and marriage to foreigners. Moreover, in the 'Survey on Social Attitudes' conducted by the Prime Minister's Office in December, 1985, almost 50 percent of respondents indicated that they were not interested in becoming friends with a foreigner, as opposed to 33 percent who said they were." Takeuchi, *ibid.*

Elsewhere, stable economic growth and a maturing society are rapidly starting to pump consumer and leisure elements into a social system hitherto structured predominantly for production and labor. If Japan was a purely capitalistic society, or one close to it, the responsive mechanisms would logically exist. Yet given Japanese society as it currently exists, it is not at all clear how Japanese corporate culture will or should respond to this new trend.

Naturally, any organization of employee leisure or consumer life in a company that functions as a base of production would aim exclusively at serving production purposes. Logically, nothing else would be feasible. The trend for a maturer society, however, calls for leisure and consumption distinct from production, and Japanese corporate society seems to be at a loss as to how to respond to this. A serious work ethic strongly linked to the base of production has worked extremely efficaciously in a society that has developed around corporate expansion, economic growth, and the catch-up syndrome. It can no longer be applied, however, once the catching up is more or less over.

As a result, Japanese consumption and leisure has come to be the domain of women and children with time on their hands, and not that of the social core of mature workers. High-class restaurants, ski areas, marine sports, music, and theater alike are primarily aimed at women and the young. A comparison of restaurants in Paris and Tokyo clearly shows this. Not only in Paris, but in New York and London as well, it is extremely rare for the young to show up at expensive restaurants and virtually inconceivable that groups of women would occupy most tables. Although the young are dressed up in formal attire and dining at the best of restaurants, the mature business manager and their salaryman are out in a small bar drinking their ration of sake and singing karaoke songs.

In any event, the existence of a generation gap in large organizations, especially companies--as evidenced by the talk of "old tribes" and "new tribes"--is not simply a question of age. It entails something more than mere generations. Of course, a growing generation gap caused by the rise of a mass consumer society is not just a Japanese phenomenon. In the United States, for example, a new framework encompassing these sorts of changes in the value system is being created. Pollster Daniel Yankelovich refers to this new framework as "new rules."[86] The problem in Japan, however, is that these changes in the value system are not taking place as dramatically as they are in the United States. Instead, the changes are subtle--and not always in conflict with the ancien regime. Lacking both the energy to create something new or the outbreak of chaos, Japan's closed system seem to be left only with the choice of lethargy and a slow defeat.

---

[86]Daniel Yankelovich, *New Rules,* (Mikasa Shobo, August, 1982).

Is it only an exaggeration on the author's part to argue that the Japanese firm today, shaken on the outside by a capitalistic challenge and on the inside by a slow demise in its corporate culture, seems to be thrust into unchartered waters without a compass to guide it?

The Need for Structural Reform

Compared to Meiji, Showa is often portrayed in a darker, more negative light. True, the Meiji period corresponds to Japan's youth as a modern state and, on average, the Meiji leaders were more forward-looking and optimistic. As the noted novelist Ryotara Shiba has written, "The optimists were men of their time, all eyes forward and ever bright. If there was blue sky or a mass of white clouds at the top of the hill they were climbing, that is all they focused on."[87]

But was it not the middle-aged managers of Showa who brought to completion the modernization set in motion and forcefully pursued by these young optimists--admittedly after some rocky interludes? And did not the Showa process of modernization, with its gradual development of a Japanese system, have a much bigger impact on global history than the early modernization of Meiji--which merely copied European and U.S. models? In other words, the Showa process of establishing Japan's model of mixed economy can act as a more general model of economic development, one of great educational value for future economic development in areas like Latin America, South East Asia, and Africa.

One of the main reasons for the generally gloomy view of the Showa period--which is actually high praise if only analyzed objectively--is the Second World War and the considerably one-sided view taken thereof. Although it was proper to reflect and criticize thoroughly the experiences of World War II in order that democracy might make a fresh start after the war, it is not correct (at least from an analytical standpoint) to turn this criticism into an indiscriminate attack on the pre-war economic and social structure. As Showa has come to a close and the Heisei era has begun with the coronation of a new emperor, it is imperative to take a cooler, more objective approach to the Showa period.

At present, the Japanese model of mixed economy or, alternatively, the Showa socio-economic regime, clearly stands on the verge of an historic turning point. In order to gain an accurate picture of this turning point and what lies around the corner, we must first be able to clearly identify where we stand at present and what sort of system currently exists. Japan is often told of the need for a distinct role or

---

[87]Ryotaro Shiba, postscript to "Saka no Ue no Kumo," *Bunshun Bunko,* April, 1978.

place in the world, but this can in no way be achieved without clearly identifying our national characteristics. This search for identity and the task of ascertaining what we can offer to the world involves finding a place for Japan consistent with our history and traditions.

Takehide Nakamura took the following look at the Showa economy:

The 60 years that went to make up the Showa period correspond to the second half of Japan's modernization, and already represent a longer span of time than Meiji and Taisho combined. Sandwiched into this period, we have had a great depression, a tragic war, high economic growth, and two oil shocks. In terms of ideology and system, we have gone from a classical capitalistic economy to a time of plans and controls, then to a mixed economic regime that is often referred to as Japan, Incorporated. Now we seem to be experiencing a revival of the classical capitalistic economy.

Despite the destruction wrought by the Second World War, economic development during this [Showa] period has gone ahead at a pace that no one could have foreseen and truly radical changes have taken place. Rapid but quiet changes . . . have taken place in industrial structure, income distribution, living standards and attitudes. A comparison of society in the early years of Showa, in the 1940s, and today would quickly highlight those changes.[88]

Although Nakamura's rough review outlines briefly the violent changes of the Showa period, I cannot agree with his proposition that Japan is really "experiencing a revival of the classical capitalistic economy." As has already been mentioned, deregulation and internationalization have made headway very quickly in the large corporate sector, and the financial sector in particular. Yet the Japanese model of mixed economy is firmly implanted, and it seems inconceivable that classical capitalism should stage a revival at this late date.

There is a global trend of breathing fresh life into old systems through the introduction into mixed economies of many more market mechanisms. America's Reaganomics and Britain's Thatcherism are prime examples. So is the disillusion with so-called "socialism" that is rife in the socialist and former socialist worlds. This is not necessarily a triumph for capitalism, nor has the world as a whole become increasingly capitalist. It is, however, not my intention to claim that an Oscar Lange type of market socialism has been achieved in Japan, but it is true that

---

[88]Nakamura, postscript to *Showa Keizaishi, op. cit.*

there are virtually no capitalists, that an extremely egalitarian pattern of income distribution has been realized, and that competition via an efficient market exists in Japan. Moreover, there should be no doubt that this system has brought about both great political and economic success.

Even though Japan did not introduce capitalistic concepts in any significant way, its market mechanisms and competition have functioned extremely efficiently. Its economic efficiency may even be greater than that of a more purely capitalistic country such as the United States, for example, and there would seem to be precious little merit in capitalizing now. In fact, such an attempt might only succeed in bringing in the disadvantages of the capitalistic system, such as a wider gap in income distribution, rampant money worship, and the vulgarization of culture, or superficial fashions, thereby accelerating the corruption or demise of the system. Such trends already exist today with the Recruit Scandal and a growing pornographic presence in the media, etc., and there is a pressing need to take a fresh look at the basic tenets that underpin the Japanese socio-economic system.

Of course, upholding basic tenets and returning to origins does not mean holding on blindly to the existing regime in toto. The systems formed and firmly implanted in the 60 some-odd years of Showa have taken a beating over the years, and many have drifted a long way from their original purpose. Moreover, because economic expansion has taken place at a rapid pace, existing interests have become incorporated into the system. Thus, rather than recognizing wider national interests, there is undeniably a strong systemic trend now toward protecting and maintaining existing interests within the status quo.

The question is whether the basic tenets of the Japanese mixed economy--in other words, anthropocentrism, or a system of true equality and participation--can be maintained as the system becomes more open and transparent in response to the trend toward deregulation and internationalization.

Itami, for one, argues the following:

> Post-war Japanese corporate society has become a different animal than capitalistic corporate society in other countries to date. It has created a classless, democratic corporate society. Hence its success. Should that not continue to be the doctrine of Japanese companies in the future? Would this not enable Japanese companies to cross both temporal and geographical borders? Yes, there are many aspects of the specific business

management system that need to change. Yet there is no need for the prototype to change, nor should it be changed.[89]

It is precisely in order to uphold the basic tenets of the system and to maintain the prototype that its antiquated parts should undergo an extensive overhaul, thereby preventing imminent decay and stagnation. Instead of trying to turn Japan into some cheap, capitalist society in the name of deregulation and internationalization, for example, bold, structural reform is required to maintain the impartiality of the public sector and the democratic features of the Japanese firm. To this end, there is a need to reexamine--in the light of their basic ideology and today's new climate--systems that have become dominated by vested interests and have lost sight of their original purposes. Yet this is a mammoth task.

In this setting, it is market competition, especially international competition and so-called *gaiatsu* (pressure from abroad), that have increasingly acted as forces for reform. It is sad in a certain sense that there has been no large-scale systemic reform without *gaiatsu*. Yet it is only normal that a stable and successful society finds it hard to harness the energy for reform from within.

In this regard, the Structural Impediments Initiative talks offer an ideal opportunity to reform the system structurally. The purpose of reform, however, is not to transform our society into a capitalistic regime, but to maintain its non-capitalistic nature while internationalizing its mechanisms. Japan and the United States, in particular, should recognize this basic difference in ideology, although the two have been converging somewhat in recent years, with Japan becoming more and more market oriented while the United States has become increasingly aware of market failures. Agreeing on differences in a liberal atmosphere seems to be the first important step toward drawing up workable joint strategies and truly sharing burdens. The Japanese search for identity and the establishment of our own legitimate position in the international community is all the more important given the new upheavals and major transformations currently taking place in Europe. Indeed, it is incumbent on Japan in such a process to internationalize and open the Japanese system to the rest of the world while retaining anthropocentrism as its basic doctrine.

---

[89]Itami, *Jinponshugi Kigyo, op. cit.*

VI. Supplement: Genealogy of Debates on the Japanese Economy

The Debate on Japanese Capitalism

In terms of its impact on the political situation at the time, the fact that the almost meaningless debate on Comintern theory pitched around the Communist Party had such a prolonged, sustained effect on Japanese intellectuals speaks volumes about the state of Japanese intellectuals since Meiji.

At the time, and until quite recently, "socialism" and "communism" were viewed in some circles as the most "advanced" of the learning or ideology imported from the West. It was very common for many Japanese intellectuals from Meiji times onward to study these theories seriously to see how they could be applied to "backward" Japan--as Nakamura comments:

> That an academic topic should become the subject of political and factional debate is in itself special. But an even more particular feature of this debate was that the battle was fought over the justness of interpreting the development of capitalism in Japan based on the assumption that Marxist economics constituted the only "social science." The issue therefore was how to interpret the facts provided by historical materials according to one's own stance on Marxist lines, and this position was a

natural premise irrespective of whether you belonged to the Koza or Rono School.[90]

Unfortunately, space does not permit a detailed analysis of the debate on Japanese capitalism, but let us briefly sketch subsequent developments starting with Moritaro Yamada's 1934 book, *Nihon Shihon Shugi Bunseki.*[91]

Yamada's "analysis" more or less represents the sum total of Koza School opinion. Yet in this work he comes up with a model system for a specifically Japanese capitalism that concentrates on the period when industrial capital is established, and has it acting as a fetter on the development of productivity, dissolving and then leading to revolution. The model system for a specific Japanese capitalism is basically regulated by the rural village, which features the semi-feudalistic landowner and the semi-serf tenant-farmer's minuscule cultivation, both being products of land tax reform in the Meiji period. On top of this rural village foundation towered the huge state-run military-related industries and material supply industries (coal, steel, etc.). These were in turn surrounded by the weaving, silk, and spinning industries, whose existence was based on low-wage labor from the rural villages and harsh working conditions. This "military and semi-serf model system" is said to have undergone its "final determination" around 1897-1907, in turn shaping Japanese capitalism in the 1920s and 1930s.

At the time, this analysis by Yamada identified the basis of Japanese specificity and thus backwardness as the completely devitalized rural village, and provided a comprehensive theory explaining the weakness of Japan's economic structure. This approach attempted to develop military and material industries from above while centering elsewhere on the textile industry (with its cottage-industry nature) and silk production (which was capable of supplementing household income). In the March 26, 1934 edition of the *Tokyo Nichi Shinbun,* Marxist economist and political commentator Tsunao Inomata reviewed Yamada's book and concluded:

> To date, the trend in studies on the unique nature of Japan's capitalism has been to place decisive importance on the semi-feudalistic relations of production seen in the early years of Meiji, and to regard these restrictions as determining the specificity of Japanese capitalism down until the present

---

[90]Nakamura, *Meiji Taishoki no Keizai, op.cit.,* p. 254

[91]Iwanami Shoten, 1934.

day. This trend has been taken completely up in Yamada's work and given its best treatment, even to the point of schematization.[92]

Yamada's mentality, with its extreme emphasis on the specificity and backwardness of Japan vis-a-vis the West, can be said to be typical of the time, or rather of intellectuals since Meiji. It is perhaps only natural that so many intellectuals despaired of the Japanese reality and were extremely pessimistic about Japan's future--for example Ogai Mori, who struggled within the establishment and put his longing for Western freedom and youthful memories into the character Elise in his book *Mai Hime;* Takeo Arishima, who tried to live between Japanese reality and Western ideology by giving away land he had inherited from his father to the tenants; and the leftists and students who flocked to anti-establishment movements during the depression and the rapidly evolving war-time regime. The pastiche of ever-pessimistic intellectuals lamenting Japan's backwardness on the one hand, and relatively optimistic practical businessmen on the other, was extremely common until only very recently.

In 1935, the Koza School argument was countered by Marxist Itsuro Sakisaka of Kyushu University in articles in the journals *Senku* and *Kaizo.* Argued Sakisaka, "There is a group of apostles and their bible is Moritaro Yamada's *Nihon Shihon Shugi Bunseki.*" He added in a separate essay, "The methods used in *Nihon Shihon Shugi Bunseki* are the opposite of Marxist methods, being those of ideal metaphysics, and their main feature is the omission of that `viewpoint' known as social development."[93]

For Sakisaka, the biggest problem with Yamada's analysis was the absence of any social dynamics. He argued that in Yamada's analysis, the "militaristic semi-serf model system" of Japanese capitalism was established around 1897-1907, and remained unchanged for about 30 years. Is it likely, he asked, that such a model created by force would go unchanged for 30 years? Sakisaka's position was that the laws of motion of capitalism itself start to work the very moment a model is created and keep working until their logical fulfillment. He maintained that although capitalism in other countries had its own special features owing to historical events and evolutionary processes, capitalism always gradually destroyed its predecessor and approximated the general capitalistic model as long as capitalism was capitalism.

---

[92]Shinkichi Nagaoka, *Nihon Shihon Shugi Ronso no Gunzo* (Minerva Shobo, 1984), p. 174.

[93]Itsuro Sakisaka, "Nihon ni Okeru Hokenteki Seiryoku no Mondai," *Senku,* October, 1935; "Nihon Shihon Shugi Benseki no Hohoron," *Kaizo,* October, 1935.

From Sakisaka's viewpoint, Yamada's concept of "semi-feudalism" or the "semi-serf" was extremely ambiguous--as indicated by the prefix "semi"--and given its denial of a farmer-formed proletariat or landowner bourgeoisie, was completely devoid of a dynamic viewpoint.

During the same period, Tokyo University economist Takao Tsuchiya and Muneyoshi Okada were also critical of the Koza School and/or Yamada's analysis. Unlike Sakisaka and Tsuchiya, Okada had embarked upon a course of practical engagement following his student days. At the time of the debate was permanent secretary at the Kanto branch of the National Farmers' Union, which was affiliated with the Social Masses Party. He was also active after the war as a outspoken supporter of the Socialist Party. As he was a practical man, Okada's counterargument was crystal clear. It pointed out that the militaristic nature of Japanese capitalism was not unique to Japan, but was rather a common feature in capitalistic countries that had reached an imperialistic stage. Moreover, the tenant-farmer system was growing apace with capitalism, which therefore made it difficult to argue about "semi-feudalistic" relations in production.[94]

Yamada maintained a stubborn silence in the face of this criticism of the Koza School except for one lecture he gave at Tokyo University in December, 1935. He was arrested on July 10, 1936, when Tokyo was still under martial law that had been declared after the coup attempt on February 26 of that same year. This arrest was part of the well-known Com Academy incident, in which leading figures of the Koza School such as Yamada and Tokyo University Marxist Yoshitaro Hirano were incarcerated. Academics of a Rono bent were subsequently rounded up in 1937 and 1938 in the First and Second People's Front Incidents, but what was most shocking to intellectuals about the Com Academy incident were the retractions made by Yamada only 10 days after his arrest and by Hirano three-and-a-half months after his. Okada speaks of the shock felt at the time:

When they heard the news, minor theoreticians of the Koza School--who had idolized him as the Big Dipper of Marxism and sung the praises of his theories as the perfect crystallization of Marxism--and some of the students who had taken his theory as gospel immediately underwent severe shock and fell into confusion.[95]

Another Tokyo University Marxist, Kozo Uno, for example, was critical both of the Koza School--for taking what was a general characteristic of capitalist

---

[94]Muneyoshi Okada, "Nihon Shihon Shugi no Kiso Mondai," *Kaizo,* August, 1934.

[95]Muneyoshi Okada, "Moritaro Yamada and Yoshitaro Hirano," *Kaizo,* September, 1936.

development in developing countries and turning it into a specific characteristic unique to the Japanese model--and of the Rono School--whose claim that capitalistic development was the same in all countries made no allowances for the special nature of developing-country capitalism.[96] He gradually developed his own "three-stage theory." In short, Uno began to seek a point of contact between Sakisaka's universality and Yamada's specificity by splitting the process of capitalist development up into a "theory of principles" and a "theory of stages:"

> Like Marx, the Marxists believed more or less that countries like West Germany, the United States, and Japan, which underwent capitalism after England, would all experience the same development as England. But when we attempt to analyze Japanese capitalism, it becomes clear that it is not as simple as that. Rather, it becomes clear that capitalism, which extends up to but does not include the agricultural industry, is an extremely exceptional case, and therefore we must consider just what that means. And having progressed as far as this point, it seems to me that the argument has to be divided into a theory of principles and a theory of stages.[97]

Thus Uno believed the problem lay in attempting to explain immediately the specificity of Japanese capitalism through a theory of principles, that theory of principles being considered as "the theory of capitalism" in the "debate on Japanese capitalism." Uno argued that Japan's specificity could be explained only by introducing a "theory of stages," holding that Japan had basically only begun its process of capitalism after capitalism had already moved on to the stage of imperialism in a global historical context. In the imperialistic stage, for example, industrialization following an increasingly sophisticated organic composition of capital does not take place quickly enough--compared with the pace of capital accumulation--to absorb employment. The result is a vast pool of latent unemployment, especially in the rural villages, and thus a great obstacle to the eradication of surviving feudalistic institutions.

Other schools of thought relatively independent of Uno's, which were shaped and developed after the "debate on Japanese capitalism," were advanced be Hisao Otsuka and Kazuo Ohkouchi, both Marxist professors at Tokyo University. As Nakamura has written, Otsuka's history was "truly a study on the development of `modern Europe'." It centered on Britain as a standard by which to verify Japan's "backwardness" and "specificity". It was probably the illegitimate offspring of the "debate on Japanese capitalism" in the sense that its underlying attitude was "how

---

[96]Kozo Uno, *"Shihon Shugi no Seiritsu to Noson no Bunkai Katei," Chuo Koron,* November, 1935.

[97]Kozo Uno, *Keizaigaku wo Kataru* (Tokyo University Press, 1967).

pathetic the Japanese reality was compared to such an autonomous and brilliant evolution as seen in the development of British `country village weavers'."[98]

Ohkouchi developed a two-tiered critique that took a critical view of social policies as part of the Marxist critique on capitalism, and also argued that, because of their specificity, Japanese social policies were not bona fide social policies in terms of total capital.[99]

The "debate on state-monopolized capitalism,"[100] which was hotly contested from 1955 to around 1970, can also be interpreted as a further development in the "debate on Japanese capitalism" during the post-war period. After all, it centered on how to rank state-monopolized capitalism in relation to the last stage of capitalistic development--i.e., the imperialist stage. Tsutomu Ohuchi, a University of Tokyo Marxist, for example, comments,

> If financial capital is still the dominant capital, in the broad sense, the present-day can also be justifiably be placed in the imperialistic stage. Today, however, capitalism is not the only system in existence and it must co-exist with, or resist, socialism. Marxist economists often refer to this period as on algemeine crise (general crisis), but in the context of global history, the only system that capitalism in the imperialistic stage can adopt is state-monopolized capitalism.[101]

In that he adopted the stance of Marxist economics, or an Uno-type "theory of stages," Ohuchi was also one of those who believed in the infallibility of logic, and who had acknowledged a certain Japanese "backwardness" as the "last capitalistic state." As Nakamura puts it:

> It is not as if the question of Japan's "backwardness" was not an issue for the Rono School or others of that persuasion. but their perception was not in terms of "specificity" because of "backwardness," but rather that this situation was "common to developing countries" because the path of development for developing capitalist countries was limited by the existence of developed capitalist countries, although admittedly it was

---

[98]Nakamura, *Meiji-Taishuki no Keizai, op. cit.*

[99]Hisao Otsuka, *Kindai Oshu Keizaishi Josetsu* (Jichosha, 1944); Kazuo Ohkouchi, *Nihon Shihon Shugi to Rodo Mondai* (Hakujitsu Shoin, 1947).

[100]Takuichi Ikumi, *Kokka Dokusen Shihon Shugiron* (1971).

[101]Tsutomu Ohuchi, et al., *Watakushi no Nihon Keizairon 2,* (Nihon Keizai Shimbunsha, March, 1966).

difficult to find other examples of this type apart from Japan. Ohuchi therefore had no difficulty in accepting high growth in post-war Japan as a phenomenon of the "post-war environment" and "backwardness."[102]

The Two-Tier Structure Theory

About the same time that Osamu Shimomura was singing the praises of high-growth policy and claiming that the Japanese economy had entered an "historical period of ascendancy," a dispute over the so-called "two-tier structure" broke out. Although it did not reach the same scale as the pre-war "debate on Japanese capitalism," it was nevertheless a weighty dispute in that it embraced not only academics but policymakers and journalists as well.

It is not an exaggeration to call this dispute the post-war version of the "debate on Japanese capitalism." Once again the focus of contention was the "specificity" or "backwardness" of the Japanese economy. Indeed, the Marxist side involved in the dispute argued that the alleged two-tier structure was not a new problem, but instead the end result of unbalanced development based on the semi-serf, semi-feudal rural village dating from Meiji times. According to the Marxists, the two did not constitute "two tiers," but were merely different sides of the same coin and therefore formed a single-tier structure.[103]

Yet it was not the Marxists of the Koza School who had advanced this two-tier theory but Yonosuke Goto of the Economic Planning Agency (EPA) in the Economic White Paper of 1957. Goto at this time was a participant in Shimomura's "inventory debate" and took a critical view of Shimomura's high-growth policies that centered on the issue of growth and cycles in the economy. Since the two-tier theory was in a certain sense a criticism of high-growth policies, the twin issues of the "inventory debate" and the dispute on two-tier structure can safely be said to have existed on the same plane for both Shimomura and Goto.[104] In other words, although high-growth policies were to be energetically pursued as the government policy of the day, there was considerable hesitation on the part of

---

[102]Nakamura, *Meiji-Taishoki no Keizai, op. cit.*

[103]Yoshimasa Kobayashi, "Nihon Keizai no Niju Kozo ni tsuite," Keizai Seminar, February, 1960.

[104]For more details on the "inventory debate" see pp. 227-312 of Osamu Shimomura's collected works, *Keizai Seicho Jitsugen no tame ni, Kohchi Kai* (December, 1958).

EPA economists such as Saburo Okita and Goto about actually emphasizing the strength of the Japanese economy as propounded by Shimomura.[105]

The two-tier structure dispute gave rise to a slight difference of opinion among government economists and ultimately developed into a theoretical debate involving Japanese academia as a whole. The participants ranged from the modern economists (the Japanese name for economists of the Keynesian, classical, or neo-classical school) to the Marxists. As already mentioned, Japanese intellectuals had exhibited a marked tendency since Meiji to lament Japan's "backwardness" vis-a-vis the West and to put forward extremely pessimistic views on the future prospects for both the Japanese economy and society. With the Japanese economy performing favorably under "high-growth policies," it is not hard to imagine why the intellectuals were reluctant to acknowledge this success--any overly optimistic interpretation could well cast aspersions on their intellectual credentials. It is in this sense that the two-tier theory provided Japan's intellectuals with some very reasonable--and convenient--counterarguments. In a way, the two-tier structure theory also provided many intellectuals with an opportunity for symbolic purification--a means of boldly reasserting their bona fides at a time when they were confronted by an extremely aggressive and optimistic economist in the form of Shimomura.

Let us now briefly run through an outline of the theory on two-tier structure as put forward by economists such as Hiroshi Kawaguchi of Chuo University and Miyohei Shinohara of Hitosubashi University.[106] Shinohara argued that the two-tier structure corresponded to the situation in a country where (1) modern and pre-modern industry existed alongside each other, and (2) a large wage and income gap between the two had been established. This phenomenon in Japan was further characterized by a discrepancy in wages according to the size of the enterprise, a concentration of small-scale operations in the employment structure, the existence of a vast pool of latent unemployed, an oligopoly, and a concentration of capital.[107]

Elsewhere, former Yokohama National University economist and current Governor of Kanagawa Prefecture Kazuji Nagasu, maintained that Japan's two-tier

---

[105]Saburo Okita, *Shotoku Baizo Keikaku no Kaisetsu* (November, 1960).

[106]Hiroshi Kawaguchi, Miyohei Shinohara, Kazuji Nagasu, Kenichi Miyazawa, Mitsuharu Ito, "Nihon Keizai no Kiso Kozo," *Shunjusha,* Vol. 1, May, 1957. See also Kawaguchi's "Futatsu no Nihon Keizairan" in the same issue.

[107]Miyohei Shinohara, *Nihon Keizai no Seicho to Junkan* (Sobunsha, June, 1961); Shinohara, *Sangyo Kozo* (Shunjusha, July, 1961,).

structure, namely the co-existence of the modern and pre-modern, was the basic Japanese structure and constitution since Meiji; that gaps according to corporation sizes (in wages, productivity, and capital intensification) were phenomena characteristics; and that behind them lay distinct, qualitative layers--the peak of which was the monopolistic company and the bottom of which was the pre-modern company. Moreover, quantitative change in Japan's economy was all filtered through this two-tier structure. In other words, expansion in employment equalled expansion of laborers at the bottom, a rise in wage levels expanded the wage discrepancy, high growth and capital accumulation heightened the gap between companies, and an increase in national income led to greater inequality in income distribution. Thus high growth policies stimulated Japan's two-tier structure, thereby adding to the contradictions of capitalism.[108]

Of great interest are the several counterarguments put forward by Ryutaro Komiya of Aoyama Gakuin University on Nagasu's theory of a two-tier structure and his theory on the Japanese economy. For after the absolute and infallible framework known as Marxism had been removed, what would seem to be only common sense deriving from an unprejudiced look at the statistics and reality sounded extremely shocking to the Marxists and even to the modern economists largely affected thereby. Nagasu, for example, writes of the top corporate leaders in Japan as capitalists. In reality, they are managers. Neglecting to analyze factual relationships, Kawaguchi rejects this assertion. Although acknowledging the distinction between the two, he insists that "The theory that a management class or the like can establish itself independently of the capitalist class is sheer deception and fantasy."[109]

Nagasu takes a more or less completely Koza position concerning the question of how this two-tier structure was formed. He analyzes it using Moritaro Yamada's logical framework while rejecting his theories of fixation and destiny. Elsewhere, Shinohara argues that although the restrictive nature of the labor market is a cause of the two-tier structure, the concentration of capital in companies is extremely important. Put another way, the state pursued a policy of encouraging the growth of large corporations, providing them with preferential loans and finance from the state coffers and subsidies. As a result of the direct link between bank capital and large corporations, an extreme bias in capital concentration towards the large corporations took place. As Shinohara wrote:

---

[108]Kazuji Nagasu, *Nihon Keizai Nyumon* (Kobunsha, November, 1960).

[109]Quoted in Ryutaro Komiya, "Dokusen Shihon to Shotoku Saibunpai Seisaku," *Sekai,* March, 1961.

If you think about it a little, Japanese financial circles before the war were comprised mainly of the *zaibatsu*. *Zaibatsu* banks were a major source of investment and funding for the large companies affiliated with the *zaibatsu*. Despite the break-up of the *zaibatsu* after the war, not only was the opportunity for reintegration created. The trend towards technical innovation and a more sophisticated industrial structure also provided a strong push for the trend towards corporate grouping, which gradually encouraged the movement towards conglomeration among influential companies. Although the ties are not as strong as in the old *zaibatsu* days, groupings between banks and large corporations can well be said to have been strengthened in response to new conditions. This trend towards capital concentration has probably been strengthened by the concentration of state funds in large corporations, mainly via the Fukkin and The Japan Development Bank. It becomes understandable why Japan's two-tier structure has taken on such a well-defined shape when this background is kept in mind.[110]

Shinohara also sought to identify the difference between the concentration of capital in Japan and in the West through "indirect financing methods." In so explaining the difference Shinohara's hypotheses has something in common with the "Japan, Incorporated" theory of Japanologists in later years.

Thus, the two-tier structure believed to have been formed in this way emerges fairly clearly in the early days of the high-growth period in the form of various statistical gaps between the large corporations and their workforces and the rest of the economy. In the dispute, however, the most hotly debated point was whether these gaps would disappear with high economic growth or continue to expand. Naturally, the government's "Plan for Doubling National Income" projected that the two-tier structure would ultimately vanish once enough growth had occurred, and that social security and welfare would also improve. Shinohara pointed out that eradication of the two-tier structure would not be easy, and would only be possible with thorough "industrial and agrarian revolutions." For Shinohara, however, this did not seem to be an imminent likelihood, but rather an ideal to be achieved in the distant future:

Whether high Japanese economic growth can be maintained in the distant future will depend on how smoothly structural shifts accompanying each of these new stages of industrialization ("industrial revolution," or

---

[110]Miyohei Shinohara, "Kodo Seicho no Himitsu," *Nihon Keizai Shimbunsha*, (November, 1961).

heavy and chemical industrialization, and "agrarian revolution," or a rapid expansion in agricultural productivity) can be made.[111]

The ex-Marxist Nagasu naturally took a very dim view of the possibility of eradicting the two-tier structure. He argued that in terms of a shortage of effective demand, in addition to problems in the overseas market, low wages arising from this structure restricted the domestic market. Therefore high-growth policies themselves were bound to fail. Kawaguchi argued unless there was rapid development in markets, especially the export market, the two-tier structure, rather than disappear, could well take on a new and different shape.

The subsequent evolution of the Japanese economy has far outstripped the forecast of the self-professed optimist, Shinohara, and the various gaps in wages, productivity, and other measures between large- and small-to-medium-sized companies that were at issue have gradually been removed. A quarter of a century after this dispute, the Japanese labor market and money and capital markets were to undergo far-reaching changes. It should be noted here, however, that these changes do not necessarily correspond to the shift--which Shinohara referred to as a "structural shift"--to a Western industrialized-economy model.

Japanologists' Theories on the Japanese Economy

It was foreign journalists and economists, the so-called Japanologists, who turned the basic proposition of Japan's "specificity" or "backwardness" upside down--along with the debate on Japanese capitalism and the argument on the two-tier structure. In its early days at least, Japanology can be said to have taken a diametrically opposed, "optimistic," and journalistic look at the "academic, pessimistic view" that had developed against the backdrop of prevailing Japanese intellectual conventions since Meiji.

The beginnings of this "Japanese theory" can be traced to Norman Macrae's September, 1962 articles in *The Economist*. Although Macrae acknowledged in this report that Japan was still a developing country, and was therefore able to achieve high-growth, he argued that the single, greatest cause of its success was that "everything Japan did was unorthodox." He praised highly several "Japanese specificities" that formerly had been regarded as some of the very symbols of "backwardness." Moreover, he referred to the economic forecasts carried out before the budget by the Economic Planning Agency, the Ministry of Finance, and the Bank of Japan as "the growth-rate forecasting game," and emphasized the impact that this "game" had on the economy via the budget. Concerning exports,

---

[111]Shinohara, "Kodo Seicho no Himitsu," *op.cit.*

Macrae also pointed out that expanding domestic demand eventually led--by creating greater production capacity--to an increase in exports. Although Japan's aggressive policy stance during the high growth period was in no way "orthodox" compared to Britain, he concluded there were not a few "lessons to be learnt."

The drift of such analyses of Japan subsequently followed two basic directions. One was the analysis and appraisal of so-called Japanese-style management, the other concentrated on analyzing government and corporate interplay, or the government role in the economic system. In the latter, the main thrust from the Japan, Incorporated hypotheses down to more recent theories on industrial policy has concentrated on government regulation and guidance of the private sector, especially by MITI.

As Eugene Kaplan of the U.S. Department of Commerce wrote in 1977:

The functioning of "Japan, Incorporated" depends heavily on what one observer has called the "rolling consensus" of the establishment which governs Japan. "Rolling consensus" is a term probably more acceptable to the authorities on this subject, who question the use of the word "interaction" to describe what occurs between government and business.

Economic decision-making is dominated by the political leadership, the business community, and the administrative bureaucracy. An often influential but somewhat lesser role in this decision making is taken by representatives from academic circles, the research institutes, and labor.

The establishment determines directions for the Japanese economy and how the goals set should be reached. Although positions of various interests in the establishment may initially differ considerably on these issues, their views are usually melded through the consensual approach so prevalent in Japan. Consensus is facilitated by the closeness of the ties linking the political leadership, bureaucrats, and businessmen. Members of each of these groups come from similar backgrounds; some even have family connections. Ties do not guarantee an immediate positive response from the others to an initiative from any one group. But all are willing to seek a generally acceptable position and to abide by the result.[112]

Taking the Kaplan analysis further, for example, Princeton University historian Cyril Black compared the economies of Japan and the U.S.S.R., pointing out that

---

[112]Eugene Kaplan, *Japan: The Government-Business Relationship* (U.S. Department of Commerce, 1972).

Japan has maintained a "corporate" type management since the latter half of the 19th century, and that as a result, the Japanese economy has combined the better aspects of both capitalism and socialism. To put it differently, Japan has achieved efficiency and harmony.[113] Chalmers Johnson devised the term "developmental state" to describe the Japanese economic system, and highly commended the role of the government bureaucracy and that of MITI in particular. He argues that Japan is a plan-oriented market economy of a type that can increasingly be found throughout Asia, including in Korea and in Singapore.

This line of analysis, which links up with current U.S. debate on the question of reorganizing the Commerce Department and/or launching an "industrial policy," upset existing theories on the Japanese economy, for it praised Japanese state participation in the market economy--something that Japanese intellectuals saw as proof of that country's "backwardness." And it called for applying some such Japanese-style practices to the "advanced" U.S. economy. These arguments were based on a frank look at the actual facts, and did not view the Japanese economy through the Marxist or neoclassical economic prism. But they diverged so sharply from the Japanese view precisely because they included considerable misreadings of the facts, which only those unfamiliar with the system would make.

It was Harvard University sociologogist Ezra Vogel's *Japan as No. 1* that had the profoundest shock on not only academism, but Japan as a whole.[114] Vogel's bestseller at first confused the Japanese and then gradually created a sort of confidence in the country, which ever since Meiji had been trying to catch up with and overtake the West. Kyoto University economist Masahiko Aoki comments as follows on the situation around this time:

It was exactly at this time [about 1979] that Ezra Vogel's *Japan as No. 1* came out, and it was a culturally symbolic event. Despite the fact that I, myself, and many experts were fairly critical of the book, those involved in Japanese business affairs and the general Japanese public suddenly realized that in many ways, especially in the economic field, that Japan had become a global front-runner, as illustrated by *Japan as No. 1*. It was in this sense that the publishing of this book was a kind of symbolic event.[115]

---

[113]Cyril E. Black, et al., *The Modernization of Japan and Russia* (The Free Press, 1975).

[114]Ezra F. Vogel, *Japan as No. 1: Lessons for America* (Harvard University Press, 1979).

[115]Aoki, Koike, Nakatani, *Nihon Kigyo no Keizaigaku, op. cit.*

In that they were the ones placed in the limelight as global frontrunners, it was individual Japanese companies or the Japanese company in general that gained a higher profile, rather than the Japanese bureaucracy or MITI.

In 1971, Peter Drucker pointed out that there was much to be learned from Japanese management, since it differed from the West's in the following ways: efficient decision-making; flexible productivity and labor costs, as well as the coexistence of motivated workers and job stability; and the fostering of many young managers.[116] Drucker's paper shared the same symbolic significance as Vogel's No. 1 theory, in that it established what aspect of Japanese management should be studied.

James Abegglen had an even earlier interest than Drucker in Japanese companies, especially in factory production-management methods, and had developed his own theory on Japanese companies.[117] In his latest work, *Kaisha*, he comments on the Japanese company as follows:

> There is another important feature in this process . . . one which forms the very basis of the Japanese company and is its greatest fundamental "strength" . . . corporate culture. Corporate culture defines hiring practices, training, motivation, and methods of generalization. It has often been pointed out that whereas the West is keyed into individual performance, Japan values group performance. Needless to say social cultural factors lay behind this difference. However, it is the Japanese company and it alone which has tapped the traditional Japanese respect for the harmony of the group for the greater corporate good and which has systemized it into the extremely familiar shape we see today in the Japanese corporate sector.

> At the same time as being the means of Japan's amazing economic growth and industrial revolution, the kaisha is also a product thereof. The kaisha is trying to apply the lessons it has learned to date in the rapidly growing domestic markets to international competition. Japanese companies share four common perceptions on business competition: 1) in a rapidly growing market, market share is a key indicator of corporate performance; 2) greater plant-and-equipment investment may lower profit margins in the short run, but . . . should be pursued energetically in line with or preferably faster than market growth; 3) prices are the greatest

---

[116]Peter F. Drucker, "What We Can Learn from Japanese Management," *Harvard Business Review,* March-April, 1971.

[117]James C. Abegglen, *The Japanese Factory: Aspects of its Social Organization* (The Free Press, 1958).

weapon in raising and maintaining market share, therefore prices must be lowered if costs fall; and 4) there must be a successive stream of new products in order to maintain a cycle of greater plant-and-equipment investment, lower costs, and increased market share.

The five key points in Toyota's production methods are small lots, few transportation operations, standardized production, lower inventory and production control by the kanban system. These elements are subtly but strongly combined to raise productivity in the factory as a whole. Worker productivity in factories using the kanban system is markedly higher than that in normal factories. There is a startling gap in overall factory worker productivity in Japanese and U.S. car manufacturing plants.[118]

Such "Japanese" terms as quality circles and kanban quickly found their way into the English language, and then into Western business administration, and were seen as the source of strength of the Japanese company and factory. Following on from *Japan as No. 1* and *Theory Z* (by William Ohuchi), Japanese companies have become the focus of global interest, with a book by one of Japan's leading businessmen based on his own experience in the Japanese corporation even becoming a bestseller.[119]

These theories on the Japanese economy and company at first can only have appeared secular and not worth serious consideration to traditional intellectuals or to Marxists, who believed that Japan's high growth was only possible because of its "backwardness." Yet as their influence gradually grew, these theories started to have a delayed but significant impact on Japanese academics. Although Osamu Shimomura most certainly stressed the inherent strength of the Japanese economy in the late 1950s-early 1960s, he was one member of a small minority. Even Shinohara, who was relatively sympathetic to the high-growth theory, clearly drew the line at Shinomura. The very fact that foreign Japanologists were necessary for a positive reappraisal of the Japanese economy and the Japanese company was perhaps no more than a true reflection of the intellectual mind-set that had prevailed since Meiji. There was, however, also a dangerous side to the overnight switch from pessimism to optimism. Observations from abroad that Japanese businessmen and the Japanese public in general have become arrogant stem from this shift in the latent awareness of the Japanese themselves, and there is a real possibility that this Japan-as-No.-1 syndrome will subtly affect Japan's future external relations--all the more so as Japan's international influence rapidly expands.

---

[118]Abegglen and Stoke, *Kaisha, op. cit.*

[119]Akio Morita, *Made in Japan* (E.P. Dutton, 1986).

Development of a New Japanese Corporate Theory

During the 1970s and 1980s, a group of Japanese analysts started reacting sensitively to the issues raised by Japanologists. These analysts were typically characterized by their comparative youth (at least at the time) and by their study or research experience in the United States. Significantly, they also represented a cross-section of economics, business administration and/or theory, and empirical research.

As a theoretician, Masahiko Aoki, was positioned at one extreme of this movement, and played a leading role. Although his thinking seems to have been substantially affected by his two research and education stints at Harvard University, it should be noted that his position is based on an antipathy for "neo-classical" economics:

> The neo-classical paradigm, which has thrived in its Anglo-American homeland and propagated to other industrial countries including Japan, reflects a rather simplistic and mechanistic view of the firm . . . . Although we will not try to present a unified grand theory of the firm in this book, all of the contributors seem to agree, implicitly or explicitly, that the modern corporate firm needs to be regarded as a coalitional association of diverse constituents, such as managers, employees, banks, investors, business partners, and so on, rather than as a mere technological black box. Or, to put it in somewhat more neo-classical terms, the modern corporate firm is a legal fiction that serves as a nexus for the bundle of long-term contractual relationships with the owners of human and financial resources as well as business partners. It may be only differences in the mode and extent of these associations, or contractual coalitions, among firm-specific resource holders that give rise to national and individual differences in the character of firms.[120]

Starting from analyses of the Japanese reality, new theory-oriented analyses--which looked at Japanese firms along the lines of Aoki's general corporate theory and pointed out the weakness of the neo-classical approach to firms--did a masterly job in overthrowing the pattern of molding reality to theory previously characteristic of Japanese intellectuals, especially Marxist and neo-classical economists.[121]

---

[120]Aoki, *The Economic Analysis of the Japanese Firm, op. cit.*

[121]Masahiko Aoki, *Gendai no Kigyo* (Iwanami Shoten, 1984).

From a business administration stance, it is Takayuki Itami who sums up the characteristics of the Japanese firm in the form of "peoplism." According to Itami, peoplism is functionally characterized by employee sovereignty, decentralized sharing, and an internalized market. Its greatest advantages are participation, cooperation, a long-term outlook, and efficient use of information:

> The idea is not to see people as a resource that merely provides labor, but as a presence with both emotions and brains, a presence that wants to express its individuality but at the same time considers harmony within the group to be natural. And the company is made up of a group of such people. By making this very obvious idea the basis of the corporate system, post-war Japanese corporate society became a very different creature from other, existing corporate societies in the major capitalist economies. It created a non-stratified, democratic corporate society. Thus its success. I believe this should continue to be the ideology of Japanese firms, which should enable them to transcend both time and borders. Certainly there are many practical aspects of management that need to be changed. But there is no need to change the underlying principle. It is better left unchanged.[122]

Coming from different directions and using different approaches, Aoki and Itami arrived at almost the same perception of the Japanese firm and proceeded to generalize from this in their own respective ways. Discrepancies do exist between the two, however, and the following is a discussion between them on this point.

Aoki: I would like to stress that the Japanese firm does not operate on the single principle of employee sovereignty. There are two principles at work, the profit principle and employee sovereignty, that must accommodate each other. This two-dimensional principle must be recognized and we have the economic tools to do so.

Itami: I don't exactly see why that is two-dimensional and why employee sovereignty is one-dimensional.

Aoki: Take employee sovereignty as an example. Why do layoffs take place when corporate performance deteriorates? In a layoff, workers who were previously the core of the company concerned are sacrificed and forced to leave. Right?

---

[122]Takayuki Itami, *Jinpon Shugi Kigyo* (Chikuma Shobo, 1987).

Itami: That can be explained in terms of employee sovereignty. In short, older workers are in fact people who have already received wages and the benefit of work for many years from the company, whereas younger workers have received them for a much shorter period. An attempt to treat these two types of people "equally" implies that those who have already received a lot leave while those who have not received enough stay on. The principle behind this explanation is "equality amongst those who are sovereign." You have been using the term profit principle as if it conflicted with employee sovereignty, but I don't believe that it does. The logic of capital has two meanings: stockholder logic and profit logic. Although I don't believe in the logic of capital in the stockholder sense, I do believe that the logic of capital in terms of profit logic is very strong in Japan. This is because of employee sovereignty. Because the firm can no longer exist as an economic entity unless corporate profits are increased, the company will go bust if those profits aren't forthcoming irrespective of who is sovereign and who receives profits.

Aoki: But as a result, Japanese stockholders in fact get a very high return. Although dividends are low, they receive a very substantial profit in the form of capital gain . . . . If they are going to receive such high returns, there is no need for the stockholder to take all the trouble and time of going to annual meetings and making a fuss. In Japan, it is the job of the banks to see whether firms are being properly managed or not. The system whereby banks have stockholdings is very specific to Japan. Banks act as monitors and the system is set up so that as long as managers can keep the banks happy, there is no need for stockholders to make themselves heard.[123]

These stockholdings of the banks are important in understanding Japanese corporate management and industrial organization. Aoki commented on them as follows:

> The role of the banks as shareholders in Japan should be understood in the broader perspective of intercorporate shareholdings . . . . Intercorporate shareholdings are substantial in Japan . . . . Intercorporate shareholding . . . has given rise to two types of corporate groupings: one is the so-called ex-*zaibatsu* corporate groups (*kigyo shudan*) or the financial *keiretsu*, in which major corporations are grouped together through mutual shareholding primarily along the old *zaibatsu* lines and/or with banks as

---

[123]Masahiko Aoki, Takayuki Itami, Kenichi Imai, "Kigyo wa Dare no Mono ka," *Economics Today,* Spring, 1988.

nuclei; and the other type is subsidiary groupings, or capital *keiretsu*, in which dominant parent corporations are connected with many satellite corporations (subsidiaries) through shareholdings and vertical relations.[124]

There has been much debate regarding the motivation behind the formation of these corporate groups, with Nakatani, for example, arguing the importance of the insurance-like role of pooling corporate risk as a group.[125]

On the other hand, in response to this logical and conceptual approach to the Japanese firm and to the framework of industrial organization, labor economists like Kazuo Koike and Haruo Shimada of Keio University adopted methods that highlighted Japanese organization at a blue collar level and labor relations by means of minute, empirical studies.

In an attempt to come to grips with Japanese labor relations within a logical and general framework, these studies set out to "demystify" Japanese labor relations. They believed that Japan's labor relations had been subject to "mischievous mystification" centering on three objects of veneration--life-time employment, seniority, and in-house unions. As Koike explained:

One method is to ask various questions at Japanese and U.S. plants. But this can only cover a small number of cases, so I also use indirect statistics. A combination of the two was used to look into promotion practices. This also ends up covering wages, since they are determined by promotion practices. The results showed that large companies in both the United States and Japan have a lot in common in that they both employ for the long term and raise technical skills through building up in-house experience. So, if you replace the term life-time employment with "long-term employment" they become fairly similar.[126]

Admittedly, in addition to taking a good, hard, empirical look at Japanese characteristics devoid of any "mystification," this method of coming to terms with the Japanese firm and labor relations being "general" rather than "specific," through U.S.-Japanese comparisons and so on, has something of the business

---

[124]Aoki, ed., *op. cit.*

[125]Iwao Nakatani, "The Economic Role of Financial Corporate Grouping," in *Ibid.*

[126]Kazuo Koike, "Naibu Soshinsei no Nichibei Hikaku--Shinpika wo Haisu," in Masahiko Aoki, Kazuo Koike, and Iwao Nakatani, *Nihon Kigyo no Keizaigaku, op. cit.*

school case study about it. It has proved extremely effective in analyzing Japanese companies in particular.

Taking this proposition one further, Shimada set himself the task of exposing the universal aspects of the Japanese firm by analyzing Japanese companies in the United States.

> Reassessing what are the really effective parts of Japanese style humanware technology gleaned from the overseas production activities of Japanese affiliated companies to date . . . the non-essential parts are all washed away in the baptism of a different culture, leaving only the universal, essential parts behind . . . . Rather than forcing the unique culture of the Japanese company onto others, the path toward greater development in the future for Japan's globalizing corporate entities involves respecting different cultures and sharing with the people of the world the fruits of technology nurtured in Japanese companies.[127]

We probably will need to respond to economic globalization while separating out the universal aspects of the Japanese economic system and the Japanese firm. This, however, represents an enormous challenge for those Japanese intellectuals who have just made the jump from "backwardness" and "specificity" to "universality."

---

[127]Haruo Shimada, *Humanware no Keizaigaku-America no Naka no Nihon Kigyo* (Iwanami Shoten, October, 1988).